Journey of the Universe
as Expounded in the Qur'an

Shaykh Fadhlalla Haeri

Zahra Publications

First Published in 1985
© 2020, Zahra Publications
Distributed & Republished in 2020
Publisher: Zahra Publications
www.sfhfoundation.com
www.zahrapublications.com

All rights reserved. Except for brief quotations in critical articles or reviews, no part of this book may be reproduced in any manner without prior written permission from Zahra Publications. Copying and redistribution of this book is strictly prohibited.

Designed and typeset in South Africa by
Quintessence Publishing
Cover Design by Quintessence Publishing

Set in 11 point on 15 point, Garamond
ISBN (Printed Version): 9781928329138

Table of Contents

Book Description i
About the Author ii
Acknowledgments iii
Foreword 1
Introduction 9
Chapter 1: Creation Begins 15
Chapter 2: The Story of Man 27
Chapter 3: Growth and Sustenance 45
Chapter 4: The Meaning of Time 57
Chapter 5: Grinding to a Halt 63
Chapter 6: The Final Collapse 79
Chapter 7: Eternal Life 91
Glossary 99

Book Description

The Qur'an traces the journey of all creation explicitly and implicitly, seeing the physical, biological and geological voyage of life as paralleled by the inner spiritual evolution of man. Bringing together the meanings and derivations of individual words, the author reveals vibrant images which the language of the Qur'an so subtly projects.

About the Author

Born in Karbala, Iraq, Shaykh Fadhlalla Haeri, comes from several generations of religious and spiritual leaders. After several years living and working in the west, he rediscovered the universal relevance of the Qur'an and Islamic teachings for our present day. His emphasis has been on transformative worship and refinement of conduct, as preludes to the realisation of the prevalence of Divine grace. He considers that the purpose of life is to know and resonate with the eternal essence of the one and only Lifegiver - Allah.

Acknowledgments

The author would like to acknowledge the help of all those who assisted in the preparation of this book, in particular Muna Bilgrami for editing it, and Molly Wietig and Hajj Ahmad Mikell for proofreading it.

Foreword

Science and Religion appear to be far apart; spheres of learning that touch only distantly at some common boundaries. If we are scientists grounded in logic, learning to interpret the world in terms of cause and effect, then religion may appear an alien, illogical pursuit grounded in an ill-defined faith in the unseen that is rarely experienced and never measurable. Conversely, if we are firm in faith in the unseen and encompassed in dogma, then science appears to be an endless pursuit of knowledge with technology as a dubious spin-off with no place for man or human interaction. There is often fear and mistrust in both camps and recrimination on both sides for the obvious failure to provide a better life for the man in the middle.

Let us step back from both of these positions and try to take a place somewhere in the middle, for the one on the middle path has both camps clearly in view. Then we can ask ourselves why the practice of religion, as it is usually perceived, does not lead to peace on earth and goodwill among men. And on the other hand, we must ask why scientific progress has not led us to peace, prosperity, and general well-being for everyone here. Let us begin with a review of scientific knowledge that is pursued for its own sake and not for immediate gain in order to get a better perspective of the method of scientific enquiry.

The sun's diurnal motion and the multitude of stars wheeling about a fixed point suggest the Earth is at the center of the visible universe and man is the central observer. But man is born with the curiosity to question and to explore. It did not take him long to realize that five wandering starts did not conform to this simple picture. In trying to account for the peculiar motion of these five planets (wanderers) he embarked on a long voyage of discovery that is characteristic of all such quests for knowledge. After many false starts and bitter arguments he was satisfied that the sun and not the earth was the center. This view soon gave way to one far grander in scope when it was shown that the sun is one of billions of stars comprising the Milky Way Galaxy and that it is displaced from the center about two-thirds of the way out towards the edge.

Now we recognize that our neighboring galaxies form a local cluster and similar galaxies are visible in every direction, scattered throughout a cosmos so vast in scale that we cannot possibly comprehend its extent in either space or time. What we now detect at the discernible boundary of the universe is the faint, cool radiation remaining from the beginning of the creation. Cosmology has brought us face to face with Creation whichever way we turn! Furthermore, the galaxies are separating at enormous speed in an exploding universe that is centered on the observer, wherever he may be.

For another example from science let us turn to what is immediately at hand. At about the same time as the exploration of the cosmos began, the current theory of matter held that ultimately everything was composed of discrete particles that combined in different proportions to account for the great variety of minerals found on the earth. The minerals were assimilated into plants which were then assimilated into the animal kingdom. The fundamental building block of matter was called the atom. It took a very long time to discover the nature of the atom but only a relatively short time to find there are only some ninety-odd different atomic species in nature to account for everything observable. Stars, sun, earth, and ourselves are all made from these few different kinds of atoms proliferated into an almost infinite variety of forms. The carbon in the pages of this book was created in the stars at an early stage of cosmic evolution many aeons in the past.

Probing into the nature of matter did not stop there since atoms differ in their composition and must be built from yet finer particles. Always spurred on by exciting possibilities dimly perceived on the edge of awareness, we have probed further and yet further into the atom in quest of the ultimate building block. It is worth noting that this science of quantum physics has come to fruition just as the most far-reaching discoveries were made in cosmology. The fundamental forces that account for the nature of matter are few in number. Science has yet to account for the nature of these fundamental forces, or fields, and is still in pursuit of the unifying field theory. If we turn from the physical to the biological sciences we find an exactly parallel acceleration in understanding, after years of slow progress and false starts. This never-ending pursuit of knowledge goes on in each and every branch of science.

Between the infinitesimally small scale of the baryons in matter and the vast scale of outer space, Man stands exactly in the center. But we see ourselves separate from what we observe like someone before a mirror. Cosmology, quantum physics, and genetics are visible and invisible worlds several times removed from the dimension of Man. We have not yet faced this question in science but it is fundamental to any unifying theory.

If we pursue science with an open mind we must surely realize that inevitably we are brought to face ourselves. The pioneers in science were humble men who gazed into vistas far beyond their field of knowledge. The great beauty and order in the Universe moved Kepler to view God as the great Geometer. Newton, who built on Kepler's work, first formulated the universal law of gravity and created an elegant language of mathematics in its formulation. He said, "I do not know what I may appear to the world; but to myself I seem to have been like a boy playing on the seashore, and diverting myself in now and then finding a smoother pebble or a prettier shell than ordinary, whilst the great ocean of truth lay all undiscovered before me." This is an eloquent, humble testimony from one of the greatest men of science who was also, in the latter part of his life, a Christian theologian.

Today we are buried in an avalanche of scientific papers that threaten to proliferate at an exponential rate and no one can review even a small fraction of this information and relate to it. It was not always thus. The philosopher and scientist Immanuel Kant, in reviewing the knowledge of his day, has commented on the seeming perfection of the universe thus, "The Universe, by its immeasurable greatness and the infinite variety and beauty that shines from it on all sides, fills us with silent wonder. If the presentation of all this perfection move the imagination, the understanding is seized by another kind of rapture when, from another point of view, it considers how such magnificence and such greatness can flow from a single law, with an eternal and perfect order."

We live in a time when almost all we know concerns the physical world. Scientific investigation moves fitfully by flashes of insight, like lightning that illuminates everything for a short distance and then leaves us in darkness with more questions unanswered than before. Pursued in isolation, science cannot possibly lead to the unifying goal of all knowledge but to endless proliferation. The ultimate questions of the origin and destiny of the universe lie always just outside our reach. The way forward from here is to turn back to revelation; this is knowledge that comes to us from the other side of time. It requires that for the moment we leave aside the scientific pursuit and suspend judgment. Now is exactly the right time to redress the balance and turn to insight, to review what has come to us that speaks of inward values, right action and ultimate reward. This is in the purview of Religion which we first posited in opposition to

Science. But now we have to see religion as a unifying way of life that links the outward and inward dimensions in man, not as an imposed ritual. it must encompass everything or it will not be effective.

Man contains within himself something of his Creator. He was born to worship his Creator in order for him to return from this outward-bound journey of separation in a state of conscious awareness. The gate to worship is through submission to the unseen and the reward for complete abandonment is perfect freedom. Viewed from this standpoint, all knowledge that moves man to unity with the Creator is useful and what separates him from his goal is to be avoided as evil and of the well-defined path. There is no way in which he can find this royal road by his own efforts, try as he may. The way is in the message of those guides who were sent in times past and who have left a record and an example for us to follow. The last of the Messengers was the prophet Muhammad, peace and blessings be upon him and his family, and the last revelation to Man is the Holy Qur'an.

"Journey of the Universe" is the story of Man's journey through creation. It is the story of an unfolding, evolutionary, inward path Man was created to follow in order to know his Lord. It is played out against the vast Cosmic background that surrounds him and reveals the subtle interplay of forces within him. It places Man squarely in the center, from which he constantly strays, and sets up the balance of right action (*shari`ah*) and right knowledge (*haqiqah*). The sole basis for this exposition is the Qur'an which is itself the master-copy of creation with nothing left out. Science, seen in the light of the Qur'an, is the revelation of Creation to Man by Man. He does nothing but read what is already written within him, for he is the central actor in this Cosmic drama. His actions can only manifest that knowledge.

The Qur'an, approached correctly, teaches by itself, for

everything in the Book is supported and reaffirmed by everything else. To paraphrase the first *ayah*, after the opening *surah*,

> Those who believe in the unseen and are in fearful awareness of Allah (God in English) and establish connection with Him and who give to others from the bounty they have themselves received know for certain this is the Book in which there is no doubt.

The Qur'an itself is the great ocean of truth that lies undiscovered before us. In "Journey of the Universe" the Shaykh has built an island in this vast Qur'anic see of knowledge so that we on the shore can build a bridge to it from religion, or from science or from wherever we may stand. Then, when we have bridged this gap between our intellectual knowledge and what is already written in our hearts we see, on looking back to the shore we left, the whole landscape of our existence from an entirely new perspective.

The creation of the Universe is the eternal instant unfolding in time. There was the "nothingness" and with the fiat of creation, "*kun fa-yakun*", the "nothingness" was split into the duality of existence, symbolized in the first Arabic letter "*alif*", the primary mark of creation that descends from God. Viewed from the other side of time, from where we stand, there was this vast creation of immense energy that flung everything into separation, which we can liken to an explosion, or theorize as the "Big Bang". But everything is from its Creator and must return to its Lord. From the effulgent flux of cosmic energy was formed the first condensation of matter, the lowest heaven of existence. Within this heaven is the first movement of the return journey, as the separated parts circle about their local center of mass.

FOREWORD

The planets wheeling about the central sun are sustained by the initial energy of creation that forced them into separation. This course is exactly determined by the balancing energy of gatheredness that draws everything back to its source. Separation is temporary and apparent but gatheredness is hidden and permanent. In this broad picture of the duality of creation, gravity is the force opposing creation. And so it is in ourselves, flung from the Garden of a former existence and ever yearning to return to that which is our home. We persistently seek to unify our knowledge because that is the message already written in our hearts.

Ibrahim Stokes

Introduction

The Qur'an is the book of *tawhid*, divine unity, the book of *la ilaha illa-llah*, there is no god but Allah. It is the direct revelation of Reality. The Qur'an illuminates the connectedness between man and his environment and the interconnectedness of all aspects of creation, visible or invisible. It expounds upon the meaning of time and the experience of man in time, although the truth from which it emanates is beyond time, for time itself is encompassed in a timeless dimensional reality.

Shedding light on man's biological passage through life, this divine revelation promises another experience after death in which time ceases to have meaning, where action is not possible, and where everything stays as it is forever – beyond time.

The Qur'an expresses the opposing aspects of finity and infinity through that most concordant language in which it was revealed, the pure and ancient tongue of Arabic. The life and culture of the Arabs was always held in a finely tuned balance between two extremes, and their language necessarily reflected this. The most startlingly beautiful flowers grew out of the harsh sun-scorched desert; the most eloquent and passionate poetry emerged from the hearts of men who daily faced the mundane and sometimes treacherous challenge of surviving in such barren, unfriendly lands. The Arab mind, with is finely honed faculty of awareness, was in harmony with its environment; and the Arabs unified with the demands their lives made on them.

The sharpness in the contrasts of opposites made the Arabic language fit for giving expression to the duality that emanates from unity. The desert night is bleak, cold, and black, while the day is blindingly ablaze with heat and light. Yet, at what point does night end and day begin? They are part of one continuous cycle.

The linguistic structure of Arabic reveals this diversity within unity. Arab, the language of primordial high consciousness, of *tawhid*, reflects the knowledge which is inherently embedded within us. The only way to gain access to these truths is to trace the Arabic words to their roots and see how all their multifaceted levels of meanings develop from one root.

In the following chapters, we shall try to explore aspects of the Qur'an that relate to the creation of this world, and take from them what is directly, commonly, and experientially meaningful to us. Examining the Arabic words of those relevant Qur'anic verses will be our major tool in decoding these truths. But because the Qur'an transcends time and man's experiences, this is inherently a very difficult task. We therefore have to approach it cautiously and with great courtesy.

We will try to extract from the Qur'an the knowledge that is already programmed within us, to glean from this infinite ocean what appeals to us as human beings who are subject to the limitations of our temporary existence. What we would like to take from the Qur'an is subject to time, so we will try to put this in a chronological order – and may Allah forgive us because time has been created by the one and only Reality Whose nature transcends time.

As creatures and products of creation living in time, we experience a natural flow of time from small to large, from embryo to child, from young to old. We see things chronologically. We are familiar with regarding time as linear – each week our nails grow longer, our beards become grayer, and so on. Although we experience its passage, time itself can only exist or be experienced if it is projected onto non-time. From the point of view of the Creator – Who is not in time but transcends time, Who is the foundation of time – the act of creation, maintenance, and destruction is part of one cycle. That Reality created what appears to be the quality of direction in time and its reverse. The Qur'an, coming as it does from the Source of creation, shows us and differentiates between early creation, man's story, sustenance, and the laws that govern this life and the final destruction. We must bear in mind, however, that the entire creation came into being by the command "Be" – an instant blown into millions of years. Therein lies the secret of life.

Allah said: "I was a hidden treasure, and I wanted to be known. I therefore, created, so that I may be known." The purpose of creation is to know God in this time zone. When life in this time zone comes to an end, that knowledge will be absolutely irrefutable because there will be no possibility of misinterpretation. In the following chapters we will try to categorize the different phases for the convenience of the reader: how creation, earth, and man came into being; how creation is sustained; the meaning of time; the signs of the end and the final collapse. There is, however, a limit to how far we can separate them. When the interlinks between the phases and states of Reality in these *ayat* (signs, verses) are clearly shown as parts of one continuous cycle, we will leave them; we cannot separate them just for the convenience of illustration. One must take the entire model and only then may one read and understand the whole creational act.

Each individual perceives his life as having a beginning and an end. In order to understand the total and true nature of existence, however, we must understand the nature of its roots or causes, and that is Allah – and Allah is timeless. "Capsules" of existence in time have come from the void of "non-time", and this is where the difficulty in intellectualized understanding lies. The true understanding of the nature of this continuum can only be subjective rather than analytical or intellectual. In essence, what we are trying to do here is to be separatist; yet we realize that this goes against *tawhid*, that divine unity which is the true nature of the entire creation.

Our purpose in these chapters is to establish a platform in the sea of ignorance and loss for those of us who spend time and energy on specific aspects of contemporary science, to see if we can extend a bridge onto this platform. In doing so, we can only depend on the openings that come to us from the Qur'an, according to the extent of our abandonment and the manifestation of the knowledge of mercy upon us. We will try to identify this platform in the hope that later on we shall meet others in scientific fields to see how their endeavors fit within the broad spectrum of reality that the Qur'an presents. This is all we can do. The Qur'an does not give us specific mathematical formulae on how matter and energy, under some circumstances, can be exchanged without any imbalance in the formula. The Qur'an does, however, give us a broad description of the whole model which exists at all times and assures us of the perfect balance in every formula in creation.

The Qur'an has always been open to challenge. It challenges one to bring forth something that is like it, but then asserts that one would never be able to do so; for it is divine and absolute whereas man's knowledge and endeavors are human, and therefore both limited and relative. The Qur'an is about the absolute, the permanent, the real behind what appears to be real – the substrata beneath the crust. Our current scientific discoveries can be changed, improved upon, expanded or negated, whereas the truths of Qur'an are forever fixed. Therefore, if you want to know whether a scientific or objective situation is true, you have to put it to the test of the Qur'an and not the other way around. This is the promise that we take from the Qur'an.

Everything is created in pairs, and every aspect of creation is based on the balance of its opposite. This fact is profoundly expounded upon throughout the Qur'an. The reality in the tablets contains everything that we can experience. The book of knowledge is one book. You cannot consider the tectonics of one specific geographical region of the earth and ignore the rest of the globe; it would make no sense. You may do that only as a preliminary step in showing how the sub-model uplifts and supports the whole model, how they connect. We are all connected; we are all subject to *tawhid*. We must only take chronology from that point of view; otherwise it will be in conflict with the totality of the Qur'an, because, in truth, in our beginning lies our end and our end contains the secret of our beginning.

The totality of the Qur'an is based on the totality of the Creator. We are simply trying to take aspects that we, as human beings, can unfold. The model we are tackling is so interlinked and multi-dimensional that beginning or end is meaningless in it. Where does Allah begin and end? The Prophet, peace and blessings be upon him and his family, says (from a *hadith*, Prophetical saying, tradition): "The seven heavens, and what is in them and between them, and the seven earths, and what is in them and between them, are no more than a ring thrown in a barren land." This shows the insignificance of the heavens and earth from the point of view of the Creator. We are in creational limitation. The Creator, however, is unlimited, and the word of the Creator is the Qur'an.

Chapter 1: Creation Begins

The entire model of creation can be found in the Qur'an. In order to see the whole model, one has to look at all the *ayat* (Qur'anic verses, signs) referring to the event of creation, for each one of them reflects a certain angle. Only then will there be an interlinked picture one can visualize.

We try to be as faithful as possible to the interpretation of each *ayah* (verse, sign; singular of *ayat*) as it arises and build upon these verses layer by layer, until we have the full picture. Imagine it as an impressionist painting in which each different brush stroke has a certain independent meaning, but if we were to look at them all together we would see that they reinforce each other – a unified picture would emerge. Each brush stroke is therefore independent and yet dependent.

The same applies to the Qur'an. To understand a certain *ayah* one must hear its resonance or see its confirmation in another *ayah* – *al-Qur'an bil-Qur'an*, "the understanding of the Qur'an is by means of the Qur'an" – and the Qur'an contains its own system of checks and balances. As one of the Imams says: *Al Qur'an yufassir ba'duhu ba'dan*, "the Qur'an explains part of itself in other parts". If there is an *ayah* that is vague or is a little hazy in its limits or application, another *ayah* will clarify or delineate it. Grasp the whole and one will then get the picture. That picture must be inherently and deeply rooted in our imagination, for otherwise we would not understand the mechanics of even part of it. However, we are its product, we are part of the picture, so how can we take a complete, objective overview of it? This must be borne in mind. It is not a simple matter of isolation where there is an observer and an observed. According to the

Qur'an, the observer is the observed. At best, the Qur'an gives us a picture through which, by reflecting upon it, we will gain inner comprehension about the nature of creation.

> Surely your Lord is Allah, Who created the heavens and the earth in six periods, and is firmly established on the throne (of authority), regulating every affair; there is no intercessor except after His permission. This is Allah, your Lord, therefore serve Him: Will you not then remember? (Yunus:3)

Rabb (Lord) is related to *tarbiyah* (education, upbringing). It is the Lord who brings up everything to its full potential. Your Lord, you Sustainer, is Allah. He created the heavens and earh. *Sama'* (sky, heavens; singular of *samawat*) is what is high – high in actuality or in value. *Yawm* is a day; a day is a sequence in time that has a beginning and an end and has its own particular characteristics. A day from the Qur'anic point of view is a period of different states. The morning is different from the afternoon, and the beginning is different from its end.

God created the heavens and earth in six different phases and then established Himself upon the throne; meaning: He took complete control over them. *`Arah* (throne or foundation) is what manifested reality rests upon. A house is not held fast unless it has a foundation. The foundation holds this creation together in its movement. *Yudabbiru-l-amr* means regulating every affair; every matter will be regulated by the one Lord who is firm in His power and has control over all things.

"There is no intercessor except after His permission." The word *shafi'* (intercessor) implies solace, compassionate intercession, additional aid. Nothing will give that support unless it is in accordance with the law, according to *idhn*. *Idhn* is permission, and its root is *adhina*, to listen, allow, hear. If God does not hear one, how can He aid him? But this is not the right way of putting it; Allah is All-Hearing. It is not that Allah does not hear it, it is man who has not been real in his calling. He has not generated the right "song".

> And they have not honored God with the honor that is due to Him; and the whole earth shall be in His grip on the day of resurrection and the heavens rolled up in His right hand; glory be to Him and may He be exalted above what they associate (with Him). (az-Zumar:67)

Man, being the highest of creation, contains the echo and the meaning of creation. He was elevated above the angels who are restricted in their channels of action, that is, angels are commanded to act only in specific directions in which they have no choice. Man, to whom angels were made to prostrate, is given that choice so that he may learn to choose the right path of action. If he chooses wrongly, he will be afflicted, resisted, and given the opportunity to recognize his wrong action both inwardly and outwardly. That recognition comes about through suffering and punishment. If he chooses rightly, he will be in a dynamic state of peace and contentment, and will realize that he is acting correctly. The tests that man is given by having choice are a preparation for the next experience which is beyond time; and the next experience will either be hellish or paradisiacal, dominated by incessant turmoil and turbulence or infinite peace, bliss, and joy.

Man in this world is given the choice. If he transgresses the laws of the Creator he will inevitably act unjustly, and eventually bring about mass injustice and disturbance. It may appear that God's will is not prevalent and that matters are out of the

Merciful's grip, but it is He Who has given man the choice in the first place. We are the children in nature's playpen. The question we must ask ourselves is: are we able to grow beyond the toys or do we continue to fight over them?

When this life ends and the universe collapses, it will be clear that everything is totally and directly in the grip of God. There will be no possibility of doubting that there is anything other than His justice, whereas in this life, it may appear that God's mercy does not encompass all. Apparent injustice is caused by man's choices and wrong actions. This is the meaning of the heavens being rolled up in His hand, where everything falls directly and completely under His command and mercy.

The phrase "will you not them remember" is repeatedly used in the Qur'an. The meaning of all that has gone beforehand is in one's inner memory bank, not in one's outer memory bank. It is an inner subgenetic remembrance that gives man the meaning of what is already within him. It is asking: "Can *you* not remember the big bang, the explosion, the meaning of which is already in your heart?" There was the order, *kun fa-yakun*, "be and it is", and creation instantly occurred from the void.

There is only Allah. We, in our clumsiness, want to understand, to physicalize, to be museum curators. We like to play God – we try to solve the cosmic jigsaw puzzles, whereas the echo of divinity is ringing in our hearts. We end up trying to outwardly rearrange and save the world; but save the world from what? Have we saved ourselves from our inner madness? That is more difficult. Instead of setting ourselves right, however, we try to save the world. Indeed, it is this echo in man that makes him impatient and impulsive. When that inner memory becomes the looking glass, the man of *tawhid*, the lover of God, will receive all the surrounding manifestations as emanating from Allah. The Qur'an is the key which can unlock the divinity within his heart by its most glorious discriminating and divine light.

CHAPTER 1: CREATION BEGINS

> Allah is He Who raised the heavens without any pillars that you can see, and He is firmly established on the throne (of authority); and He made the sun and the moon subservient (to His law); each one pursues its course to an appointed time. He regulated every affair, making clear the signs that you may be certain of meeting your Lord. (ar-Ra'd:2)

This description is of the beginning of creation. *Rafa'a* is to lift up; it implies that there was an outward expansion or an outer explosion. God lifted the heavens without visible support. The forces that keep the cosmos in balance are invisible, and we only know of some, such as the gravitational, centrifugal, and electromagnetic fields. *Thumma-stawa `alal'arsh*, then He establishes Himself on the throne, the foundation from where He controls Creation; meaning that as this creation came about, its control was in His hand.

> And He it is Who spread the earth and made in it firm mountains and rivers, and of all fruits, He has made in it two kinds; He makes the night cover the day; most surely there are signs in this for a people who reflect. (ar-Ra'd:3)

Now we come to another level. The first one was about the heavens being lifted up without the aid of any visible pillars. Then we come to the earth: Allah spread the earth out. *Rawa si* means unshakable mountains. Its root word means to be firm, to be stable, and to anchor. *Marsan*, from the same root, means a port or anchorage. There is, therefore, an implied connotation of fluidity: Mountains "floated" on the molten rocks and came to rest after the cooling period of the earth. *Anhar* are rivers. The word derives from the same root as day, which means to gush or stream forth – day springing from darkness, rivers gushing from the darkness of earth.

"And of all fruits" – fruits are that which we can taste. Fruits are manifestations of all types from which we can benefit, enjoy, and use as aids in this journey. They are the final stage before decay, the final results of a plant's labor before it is recycled. Every type of fruit has been made in pairs, *Zawjayn*. He created opposites for everything one can visibly or invisibly conceive of, such as taste: for every sourness there is sweetness.

Again we are given an example of the more visible things that dominate our lives: "The night cover(s) the day." In Arabic the description is of how the night covers the day like a skin. *Ghisha* is skin, something that covers and hides.

"Most surely there are signs in this for a people who reflect." The signs are all there if only we contemplate the meaning of these forms and the cause of these effects, if only we look into their further meanings rather than into their immediate physical impact upon us.

> And in the earth there are tracks side by side and gardens of grapes and coral and palm trees having one root and (others) having distinct roots – they are watered with one water, and We make some of them excel others in fruit; most surely there are signs in this for a people who understand. (ar-Ra'd:4)

Here we are given the example of earthly systems on a physical level. There are pieces of land on earth that lie next to each other and gardens which contain similar or dissimilar plants with tap or diffuse root systems. All of these differences that we can physically observe on this land are nourished and sustained by

CHAPTER 1: CREATION BEGINS

one water. From it will come bitter or sweet poisonous or health-giving plants. Everything has its use in this world. Its ecology is a complete fiber, a complete network. Some are preferred over the others from the point of view of the *Rabb* (Lord). Some of them are right for us under certain circumstances, while others are not. As human beings with our own *dhawq* (taste), we sometimes prefer one fruit to another. We taste them differently and yet their water is one, that is, they are fed by one source. We use our `aql, our reasoning, if we can understand that all of this diversity is physically based on one feeding source, then "most surely there are signs in this".

> The Sun and the moon follow a reckoning. And the herbs and the trees do adore (Him). And the heaven, He raised it high and He made the balance. (ar-Rahman:5-7)

Everything has been made according to a plan and measure, a *qadr*. The Qur'an says: *Inna kulla shay`in khalaqnahu bi-qadr*, "surely We have created everything according to a measure" (*al-Qamar*: 49). Some of these measures are visible and quantifiable, like the orbital paths of the sun and the moon, while some of them are not, such as the time when they will come to an end in the big collapse.

Everything is in prostration to Allah. Everything is magnetized in a certain direction. Whether that magnet is faithful and points north or south as it should or is distorted in its orientation is a secondary matter. All things are already programmed to acknowledge their beginning and end and the laws that govern them.

Was-sama`a rafa'aha implies that in the early stages of cosmic expansion, creation was tight and unexpanded. Creation was dense, concentrated into a dot. Elsewhere the Qur'an says:

Khalaqa-s-samawati bi-ghayr `amdin tarawnaha, "He created the heavens without pillars as you see them" (*Luqman*:10). This statement implies that the heavens were not really lifted but were exploded, opened out of their compactness, according to a measure, a certain balance, the *mizan*.

> Do not those who disbelieve see that the heavens and the earth were closed up, but We have opened them; and We have made of water everything living, will they not then believe? (al-Anbiya':30)

The voice of truth calls us from within ourselves, from the seat of our faculty of discrimination. Do those who deny – those *kuffar* (deniers), who cover themselves up as if that knowledge is not also deeply ingrained in them – not see the truth of the one source behind every manifestation and the one essence behind every attribute? Do they not comprehend, do they not witness that "the heavens and earth were closed up but We have opened them"? This *ayah* refers to the early stages of creation when there was what might have appeared as a uniform mass – thin gas. The two aspects of our creation (heavens and earth) where connected and then were split along a certain seam. *Fataqa* is to tear a cloth at its seam, to rip apart. This means separation was already destined to happen. The seam of garment is inherently the easiest place for there to be a separation.

The meaning of *qadar* (related to *qadr*) is, therefore, divine predestination. Before anything bursts out into existence, it is set on a predetermined path. The heavens and earth were connected, but there was a boundary that was not visible along which they split. That determination was mathematically inevitable.

Here we encounter a vast, broad-brush treatment of the movement of time. The *ayah* then says: "and We have made of water everything living". Everything that has sentience has been made from water. Creation is based on the most dynamic common denominator, which is fluid – water. Indirectly this *ayah* is asking us, "Do you still not trust? Do you not believe in the one and only, all-engulfing, all-encompassing Reality? Do you not see that this is how it all came about?"

Many a living form has a rigid structure (bones, etc.) as well as a rigid outlook, and yet, even physically, its foundation is subtle. This, too, is based on something subtler, the condensation of a gas, which in turn, has a subtler foundation that is undiscoverable scientifically but is recoverable by those who submit to the sea that contains all and who dive into it.

> And We have made great mountains in the earth lest it might be convulsed with them, and We have made in it wide ways that they may follow a right direction. (al-Anbiya':31)

We have seen an *ayah* similar to this one before. It is a reference to how the earth became firm and apparently stable. The mountains have been made the earth's point of anchor. Once they were settled, the open tracts between them made it easy for one to find one's way in this world.

> And We have made the heaven a guarded canopy and (yet) they turn aside from its signs. (al-Anbiya':32)

The canopy of heaven is held aloft, is preserved in its destiny by the knowledge of the Creator. But the people who are not in *iman* (trust, faith) turn away from these signs.

The heavens symbolize the limits of observable systems. Clearly it is futile and a folly to attempt to understand what encompasses a system unless we go beyond that system. In order to go beyond the systems that we can experience, we must take a quantum leap; we must abandon and submit. To understand the meaning of life, we must penetrate its boundary, which is called death. The outer cosmic system can be comprehended if the Creator is comprehended.

> And He it is Who created the night and the day and the sun and the moon; all (ones) travel along swiftly in their celestial spheres. (al-Anbiya':33)

Night and day, sun and moon were each created in a predetermined cycle or orbit – "their celestial spheres". *Sabaha*, the root of *yasbahun*, is to float or swim. *Sabaha* is to glorify or praise. They relate in that by letting oneself submit and unify with the total current of creation, one will naturally want to express wonder and to glorify Him, just as the sun and moon glorify God by being true to their destiny.

The Qur'an says that whatever is in the heavens and earth glorifies Allah; meaning, is loyal to its prescribed path. Every created entity announces its nature and is true to it. Man is also true to His Creator in that he will never rest until he discovers his real Lord. By submitting to Him, he is freed. All pursuits, whether high or low, mental or physical, are steps towards that discovery. Man is programmed to seek contentment and peace, not realizing that his real nature is already that. He thinks that he can bring about contentment and peace by satisfying desires and strengthening attachments. What he is really attached to are the Lord's attributes – *al-Hayy, as-Samad, as-Salam* (the Everliving, the Everlasting, the Everpeaceful).

Glorification implies devotion, connectedness, and therefore *tawhid*. The electron has no choice but to be loyal to its path and the changes that occur therein, according to the variations in circumstances. In that sense, we can say that it is totally devoted to, and therefore worships, its reality. In the same way, man is a creature of devotion, adoration, loyalty, and therefore worship. He seeks and therefore he is sought. If he does not seek along the prescribed path of knowledge, he will be sought by afflictions, troubles, and tribulations which are all natural ways of reminding him to bring himself back to the path of *tawhid*, through experience and knowledge.

Chapter 2: The Story of Man

> Read in the name of your Lord Who created. He
> created man from a clot. (al-`Alaq:1-2)

The Qur'an reflects the signals which echo in man's heart. The clarity of the echo is proportionate to the purity of the heart, and that is the meaning of the command to read.

The origin of man is the command of God – Be. The *ruh*, the spirit, is like a subtle force, the origin of which is in another realm and cannot be directly experienced or intellectually understood. The presence of such a force is indicated by the experienceable manifestation it causes. A divine breeze causes the coagulation of the first cells, which then derive nourishment from the earth of the womb and move through the various stages of growth into a discernible form. Man was formed in such a way as to enable him to reflect upon his true origin.

In Arabic the root word of *ruh* (soul) is the same as that of *rih* (wind, breeze) and *rahah* (comfort, ease). The search for comfort and ease is ingrained in man's nature. The subtle force that results in the creation of man is divine, sublime, and indiscernible by our gross intellects. The power of the intellect is derived from the *ruh* so how can it directly comprehend the nature of its originator? The Qur'an explains the origin of the *ruh* as a command – an instant of creation.

Man is in physical growth, and if he does not accompany that with spiritual growth he will then be out of balance. Physical growth signifies a cycle of stabilization and maturity and a return to the physical origin, the earth. Spiritually, the *ruh* rises from the unseen and is captured in the body, seeking its source by upholding and desiring the attributes of its creational source – harmony, peace, independence, contentment, etc. – and eventually returning at death. It is as though the body is loaned by the gross earth to the subtle *ruh* for it to discover and know its Creator so that it knows its own nature, and thereby knows the right courtesy of gaining access to Him and getting close to Him, before its promised return – death.

That loan will be a successful one if the path of abandonment, of Islam and *tawhid*, has been followed in this journey of life. After death, other processes of purification and neutralization, such as the fire and the garden, are part of the process of bringing the *ruh* to acknowledge its origin. Man is therefore physically sustained only for him to recognize his original state, and his original state is to be in true submission and abandonment.

> The Beneficent God, taught the Qur'an. He created man, taught him the clear evidence. (ar-Rahman:1-4)

The mercy (*rahmah*) of Allah pervades everything. The Adamic state of being in the garden was one of complete bliss and tranquility; there was no hardship. God's advice to Adam, for it was advice and not a command, was not to go near that tree of turmoil, jealousy, and discontent. If it had been a command, Adam would have obeyed it because at that stage the Adamic consciousness knew only obedience and truth. It had no discrimination because it had not experienced untruth, until, that is, the rise of *shaytan* (Satan, the devil).

Once Adam tasted the "fruit" of the tree, he had to go through the full process of learning discrimination, which comes about by being exposed to opposites. The descent to earth was a natural outcome of the process of guidance. The earth is man's arena of practice where he can exercise choice and learn to select the right course of behavior and action. Man has inherited this knowledge from his primal state when choice did not exist.

Man was told: be in the garden and you will be in complete bliss – a state of positive neutrality. You are the closest to the Creator, but do not venture near that *shajarah* (tree or bush). Here we would not translate it as "tree". The root of the word is from *shajara* (to happen, break out, and in other forms, to quarrel, fight) and is related to *shijar*, fight or quarrel. *Shajarah* implies upheaval. The warning to avoid that tree implies avoiding that state of questioning which causes man to be in uncertainty and upheaval. The moment he asks, "Why am I here?", he shows his impertinence; for were it not for the grace of life within him, he would not even be able to ask the question.

The tree of desire and expectation arose when Adam was told, "don't", and he asked, "why?". It is in the nature of the beast, for he contains the exception, which is *shaytan*. If we allow that state to predominate, the exception will be the rule, as it is now in the world.

A river has the main characteristics of viscosity and flow. The molecules of water that lie on the river banks are immobile. The rule is the mainstream, but the exception defies the mainstream. The rule is the abandonment into the natural creational laws, and the exception, we are reminded, is that there will be opposition. The rule is that a child is conceived out of intercourse between a man and woman and the exception is immaculate conception. As we know, this exception occasionally occurs and did in the case of Sayyidna 'Isa (Jesus). This is the *sunnah* (way) of creation.

The mercy of Allah is always there, and it is this mercy that enables Adam to return to that state of bliss. He returns when he recognizes the mercy. The knowledge of the Book of creation is the first and most encompassing manifestation of that mercy – and that knowledge implies the knowledge of *tawhid*, the divine unity behind diversity, the unity of good and bad, the garden and the fire.

Adam was taught this knowledge. The knowledge was subgenetically ingrained in him. That is why the angels protested the creation of man who was going to squander his wealth and shed his brothers' blood. God taught Adam the knowledge of *furqan*, discrimination, the knowledge that comes from *shaqa'*, mercy and wretchedness. Man encompasses the meanings of all the divine attributes.

Adam remained in primal undiscriminating bliss without being tormented by opposites until he unwittingly transgressed the bounds. Adam knew the conditions for remaining in the garden, but desire was encouraged in him. The conditions of unquestioning, desireless tranquility and bliss excluded desire, and by desiring he was made unfit for the garden.

The rise of that desire – wanting the taste of the tree's fruit, wanting its meaning – heralds the birth of understanding and choice. As a consequence, man experiences differing outcomes of his discriminating actions which will result in his claiming of his heritage and original abode, the garden. Following the whispering suggestions of *shaytan* (from the verbal root *shatana*, to be cast off, e.g., a path) will, however, result either in man's waste and destruction, or in his recognition of the bounds. By recognizing the bounds, he remains within the garden walls, content with submission and *tawhid*, as he was in his original state.

Man was created with total potential. He was created in order to be the hand of Allah, the eye of Allah, the ear of Allah, and to be in bliss. His consciousness arose by the fall from which his rise occurred. Consciousness of consciousness arose by him asking "why not?", by wanting to know, that is, by testing the fruit of the tree. Immediately after that he was caused to descend to the earth, the scene of future experiments. In other words, man contains the highest elements within himself, but in order to get to them he must first reconstruct himself from the bottom upwards. That is why we say man must go down to his lowest level, his foundation, in order to recognize the enmity within himself. Half of man is fighting, trying to demolish the other half; half of him is doubting and the other half inclines to *iman*; half of man is trying to see the mercy in everything and the other half is full of selfishness. Man must reconstruct himself from the lowest level so that he can rise to the highest level already within him.

The start of that reconstruction begins with doubt, with questioning the meaning of the tree. The eating of the fruit of the tree symbolizes the alienation arising from the split between the angels and *shaytan*. *Shaytan* said, "I am better than him", and so Adam said to himself: "I am qualified to ask. Why should I be deprived of thinking, of questioning, of my mind or my attachments?"

> There surely came over man a period of time when he was a thing not worth mentioning. Surely We have created man from a small life-germ uniting (itself): We mean to try him, so We have made him hearing, seeing. (al-Insan:1-2)

Man is forgetful. Even while diligently seeking, we forget some basic lessons we have learned along the way. Similarly we cannot remember our state in the womb. We cannot remember how we were created or how we grew in those nine months of darkness. Before that, no one could even talk about us; nobody knew of our existence because we were in the unseen. These *ayat* remind us of that time when we could not be mentioned. What is meant is that there most certainly was a time when we were in the unseen, when we were hidden in the knowledge of God, when nobody knew that we were likely to come into this existence. Our existence was in another realm, one that we could not talk about or experience. That is why we say that this knowledge was with Allah, for His knowledge encompasses the visible and the invisible and the laws that govern this existence and the unseen.

Everything was once in the non-time zone that now manifests itself in time. Marriage and intercourse, for example, are divine actions because we are interacting with and being the interspace with the unseen. The correct courtesy in approaching intercourse is to invoke the divine name: *Bismi-llahi-r-Rahmani-r-Rahim*; "In the name of God, the Beneficent, the Merciful." One is entering a zone of the unknown. One does not know anything about this *ruh* that may result or what its nature will be. He has no idea. There will, of course be many connecting elements – physical resemblances and inherited characteristics – but ultimately it is yet another being. It is quite a different entity, one that asserts its individuality. It has all these interlinks with the seen, but it also has links with the unseen, with Allah.

Elsewhere in the Qur'an Allah says: *Alastu bi-rabbikum?* "Am I not your Lord?" (*al-A'raf*:172). When the experiencing of one's own self stops, the experiences of one's real self take over. By posing this question God is asking, "Why were you separate from Me, why did you not believe in My mercy, why did you not abandon yourself to Me? How did you forget? How could you forget? What is your excuse?" On the Day of Reckoning, when all excuses and props are meaningless and useless, man will see that he has no excuses.

Man was in the unseen, with Allah in a pure state, and has come here in order to have the distinction and the honor of recognizing this pure state. In a sense even to have the possibility of saying that he is separate, or of seeing that some sort of Lordship exists, is like playing God. Ultimately, when time stops for him, he will enter a zone of non-action. In order to elaborate on the magnificence of this situation, he is also reminded that there was a time when he was also unable to act, to do anything in the womb.

Inna khalaqna-l-insana min nutfatin amshajin. Man was created from a dot of a cell, from a liquid, from the lowest thing in existence. The smallest atom in existence is hydrogen, and once hydrogen is oxidized, it starts to decay and becomes water. All creation is based on water. We decay as we grow. In other words, we have been created from the tiniest, most insignificant, decaying thing. The magnificence of the Creator's divine being hides, in a sense, in that form.

Nabtalihi is derived from *ibtala*, which means to test, afflict, and wear out. *Thiyabun baliyah* (*baliyah* and *ibtala* come from the same verbal root) are clothes that are threadbare. We are tested so that what is not is worn off us. We are tried in order to recognize that all the accoutrements of life are of little value. Nature's way is to make us wary of our desires.

The first thing man physically experiences in the womb is sound, and then after he is born, he begins to experience sight. Allah alone is the all-Hearing and all-Seeing. Man can hear and see by the mercy and grace of God. If he uses his hearing and sight in order to recognize the perfection of God, then hearing and seeing are divine acts.

> Certainly We created man in the best form. (at-Tin:4)

Man has been created in the most beautiful and perfect form. *Taqwim* (form) is from the verbal root of *qama*, to be built. Man's potential is higher and greater than all other creatures because it is divine. If *tarbiyah* (upbringing, education) and the worship of the *Rabb*, the Lord, takes place, then he is bound to experience the fulfillment of his potential. The choice is in man's hand.

> And He taught Adam all the names, then presented them to the angels; then He said: Tell me the names of those if you are right. (al-Baqarah:31)

Adam's status is higher than all angels. As a man he has more knowledge plus the gift of what appears to be choice – the choice of acting independently or dependently. By dependently we mean according to the laws that govern existence, according to the *sunnah* (way) of Allah. All the angels and all the other powers in existence were made to be subservient to the Adamic entity.

Man's indisputable and primary purpose in this life is to be healthy and content. For that to come about, he must go through a hierarchical order of stages. The first levels deal with the environmental and physical conditions: man needs shelter, clothing, food, good health. Then he needs stable mental and emotional health. After that, he can move towards the higher planes of the intellect and spirit to reach a point of highly developed inward sensitivity which will make him want to be in the most tranquil and balanced situation.

The physical and the spiritual interlink. Sustenance and maintenance begin at the physical level and end at the inner intellectual and spiritual levels; they cannot be separated. If man starts from one, he will end up at the other. If he is by nature a spiritual being, he will end up caring for his physical environment, his neighborhood and country and all of mankind and creation. If he starts from the physical level, he will end up at the spiritual. Man is a unified creature; he has both inward and outward aspects to his nature.

His sustenance and maintenance involve all of these aspects. They physical aspects of existence generally prevail, in that if one of them is off balance then the available attention and energy go towards putting it right. Once it is put right, there can then be movement along the other levels of the hierarchy – he can move into the right company and so on – until he reaches a point, usually referred to very unscientifically, of having the right "vibes" or the right "chemistry". We often use such words to describe intangible feelings. All of them mean that the reasons for the harmony between individual A and individual B are not easily definable or tangible; they are, however, important. Nobody denies their importance, but what they are cannot be clearly expressed.

Man's ultimate purpose in sustaining himself is for him to reflect and move towards fulfilling his subtle, spiritual sides. The purpose of maintenance is to give him the opportunity to reach that point where he is able to reflect, to remember, to really see that he is journeying along routes that have already been mapped. Outwardly, the path of expansion and ultimate contraction on the cosmic map is decreed. Inwardly, the highways of correct action are bounded by the warning signs of transgression, disharmony, and unhappiness. Provision and sustenance can enable man to realize that the beginning and the end have already taken place; for he contains the knowledge and experience of them subgenetically, in his inner recesses. If his life is not for this purpose, then it is nothing but a dislocated chain of events, abstractedly floating in time with no connection to anything in particular.

The Qur'an makes the purpose of man's existence very clear. *wa ma khalaqtu-l-jinna wa-l-insa illa li-ya`budun*, "And I have not created the jinn and man except that they should worship Me" (*al-Dhariyat*:56).

The real purpose of creation is to know the true meaning of `*ibadah* (worship); and the word in Arabic implies complete harmony, the absence of resistance or friction. The verbal root of this word in one form is `*abbada*, to make smooth. Through `*ibadah* life becomes smooth and therefore it will be completely connected and unified. The journey becomes only an experience rather than an end in itself; it becomes a means to an end.

> O you men! Surely We have created you of a male and female, and made you tribes and families that you may know each other; surely the most honorable of you with Allah is the one among you most careful (of his duty); Surely Allah is Knowing, Aware (al-Hujurat:13)

Creation on this earth is based on groups. When man started to unfold and awaken here on earth, his nature was markedly that of a gregarious gatherer. He is still tribal and ethnocentric. He likes the security of the same type of people, of kinship, of the same language and culture. Creation on this earth is based on tribes, nations, and the extended family. This *ayah* reminds us that increase in size and number is not necessarily the right gauge or measure of the degree of one's bliss, joy, or freedom. The real measure of this is *taqwa*, fearful awareness of falling into the trap into which it is possible for all us to fall. That trap is eating the fruit of the tree of turmoil, anxiety, attachment, expectation and jealousy, without learning from it. From that transgression and failure, man's faculty of reason and discrimination is nourished. His choice and resolve become decisive, and he learns the rules of safe conduct along his journey. How could nature be a more perfect teacher?

From the one comes two. God says in the Qur'an: "I created you from one self." Whatever man contains, woman also has within her and vice versa. How could he otherwise understand her compassion, passion, gatheredness, and especially her desire to maintain immediate existential factors in equilibrium.

The fall of Adam is the beginning of his real rise, a rise that is constructed step by step in order for him to attain his full potential. From the creation's point of view, Adam's potential is to have everything. He was told to give the angels the names, that is, to show them the knowledge of everything. The angels have their own wave band beyond which they cannot go, whereas man has access to higher knowledge.

The Adamic inner core is the visible light from the invisible *ruh* (spirit, soul). Think of the *ruh* as being the invisible power that comes from one source. Once that *ruh* becomes your *ruh*, it takes on a unique coloration. Each *ruh* at that point is given the opportunity to ascend again into the garden of complete and utter intelligent abandonment, detachment, and recognition of *faqr* (true poverty) – recognition of *la hawlah wa-la quwwata illa bi-llah* there is no way or strength other than by Allah.

In order to attain this state, man must first pass through various afflictions. First is the rise of "I-ness", of arrogance, the kind that makes one defiantly ask, "Why can't I?" Second is covetousness – "Why can't I have the fruit of this tree?" The third is jealousy, as in the example of one son of Adam killing the other. The rest follows, with one question leading to another, until man is swept into the flames of fire by his own inner fire which he inadvertently stokes.

First there was oneness. Then discernment and separation began to occur in the physical creation. Man was separated from a state of bliss and sent into a state where discrimination (*furqan*) was the key to balanced living. He was removed from a stream of primal, undisturbed, indiscriminate bliss to the consciousness of different states, in order for him to perfect his choice through the growth of the faculty of reason. What else could he choose but to return to the state of the garden?

The rise of consciousness can be understood if one considers, for example, the phenomenon of pain. Man is conscious of his pain, yet he is also conscious of the consciousness, because he can differentiate between greater and lesser pain. The light of awareness illumines that consciousness within him, and that light must be ever-glowing.

> And know that your property and your children are a temptation, and that Allah is He with Whom there is a mighty reward. (al-Anfal:28)

The nature of man as described in the Qur'an is to be a collector, a gatherer; he wants increase and goodness for himself and wants to avoid badness and filter out anything that might cause him disharmony. That disharmony might simply be in his mind or in his desires, without having a physical reality to it. Nevertheless, every human being wants equilibrium.

As part of the props that give one the assurance of continuity, stability, security, and longevity, man has his possessions and immediate dependents. The *ayah* here warns us about them so that we recognize or come to see that one's wealth is merely a filter, giving one the power to have things that he likes and are beneficial, and to avoid the things that he dislikes and are harmful. It gives him the protection, so to speak, needed to try to recreate a garden-like situation here on earth.

Our offspring are also a sign of wealth, power, growth, and increase. The Qur'an warns us that they are a *fitnah*, a test in order to unveil reality. They are there to echo the ultimate garden, the ultimate state of freedom, detachment, and timelessness which one will experience after death. Man's worldly blessings are tests to see whether he will fall into the trap of trappings. *Dinar maftun* (*maftun* is from the same root as *fitnah*) is a gold coin whose authenticity has been tested and found to be true. *Fitnah* arises when an outer agency interacts with a system or an entity thereby revealing its state or nature. It is an affliction, a test, making the truth evident. All of these worldly trappings, then, are there to rub and test man. They are the carborundum against which his metal is rubbed and polished in order to reveal its true nature and the true nature of man is divine.

If children and wealth show how selfish and dependent one is on them rather than God, then that test was successful. One can then move on, higher and higher. The testing is not to condemn man to failure or success, but to highlight his state. If he loves his child and he or she falls ill, the parent becomes miserable. That test reveals to him his attachment – and the degree of it – to this false and temporary situation. All these objects and relationships are only there to increase his awareness of his own state. The more he is tested, the more he recognizes his true state.

Ultimately, one's true state is complete abandonment and submission, and that is the ultimate salvation and awakening. The trappings of this world and the attachment to them, the tests and affliction that come with them, are for one to recognize the cause of the turmoil and the toil. Man will always toil; it is his nature. He toils towards that inner state of complete acceptance, tranquility, peace, and abandonment. If that toil is seen in the right context, then all its ups and downs reveal to him his nature, both the lower and the higher aspects. What matters is not the outcome of the outer situation but its interpretation, and that should be his joy.

In other words, the man on the path, as he is alluded to in this *ayah*, is he who sees the laws of creation within the blessings that Allah bestows on him and who simply, courageously, and genuinely observes himself. He sees, for example, that whenever he is given a gift he loves it; whenever he is being criticized, even by a friend, he dislikes it because criticism contains a warning of discontinuity which man does not like. Discontinuity means disruption, and thus the unification between actions is broken. We do not like action to be broken up even if the actions were of the wrong sort. We all reflect and look for *tawhid*. *Tawhid*, however, is to be found equally in degeneration and decadence as it is in correctness and righteousness. Birds of a feather flock together regardless or whether they are good or bad.

We are all slaves of *tawhid*. We all seek the intertwined ecology of unification. It could either be the ecology of decadence or of regeneration, and either one would recycle itself. The decaying swamp has its own perfect ecology, with everything breaking down into smaller molecules and eventually letting off gases. The growing plants in spring also have their own ecology, where the mineral of one dead plant feeds the new plant so that it may grow to maturity and full beauty.

We have the choice of being in the swamp or of being in the garden of inner growth. The *karam*, the generosity of God that always pervades everything everywhere can be recognized in a total sense when one is cautious and aware of the two dimensions within oneself, one being divine, the other being animalistic and base.

In this life we experience tranquility and joy, as well as disruption and sorrow. Life's scales oscillate between these two extremes. The *fitnah* enables us to remain in the center, discerning and experiencing the extreme ends without being swung up or down. it helps us remain in a state of spontaneous awareness, and from this comes gratitude and contentment.

> Surely man is created of a hasty temperament;
> Being greatly grieved when evil afflicts him, (al-Ma'arij:19-20)

Man is always restless and anxious. If something good comes to him, he keeps it. He hides his success fearfully, and, in doing so, he goes against the *sunnah* (way) of Allah. "If you are grateful, I would certainly give to you more" (*Ibrahim*:7). *Shukr* is gratitude. When one is in gratitude, one's heart is empty. When his heart is empty it can then breathe the eternal song that is written in it.

> Does every man of them desire that he should be
> made to enter the garden of bliss? (al-Ma`arij:38)

In this world, man will be rewarded according to his intentions, and in the next he will be exactly as he was at the point of departing this existence. If his intentions are pure, simple, and free, he will soar; if not, he will plummet downward. Gravity, so to speak, will prevail and he will have to go through a process of purification by fire or even by the garden. Many of our learned masters describe the situations in which good people go to the fire in order to taste it, to burn, and be purified. There are also those who go to the garden in order to go higher and higher within those states that being in the garden brings. The experience of the fire and the garden may well be part of a process of purification whereby the *ruh* (soul) becomes fit to attain its highest state.

Sayyidna `Isa, upon him be peace, once related a story saying: "I came upon a people who were praying for fear of the fire. I told them, you will be saved and given what you want. I came upon another people who were worshipping and praying for the garden, and I assured them that they would find what they sought. I then came upon worshippers who prayed neither out of fear of the fire nor out of desire for the garden, but out of gratitude and contentment, and they were my people." We will become the realization of our intentions and actions; and the reward of our actions will be as good or as bad as our intentions.

It is clear in all the *ayat* of the Qur'an that if we take their meanings further, we will reach a point where we are given a description of the end, of the big bang, of how the expansion of the cosmos reaches its finality. Whatever is created will be destroyed. Everything in creation is in dynamic flux, and anything in the mode of dynamic flux will come to an end; it may be that it will enter other modes. Whatever is in growth will reach a point of maturity and will decline. There can be no stagnation in creation.

It is the same for the subtler aspects of creation, such as the levels of consciousness. Consciousness will increase, rising higher and higher. That is why we say there is no stopping the people of Yathrib (Madinah). The name Madinah is based on *dayn*, obligation, debt; *madaniyyah*, from the same root, means civilization. Madinah is the place where one exercises the *din* (from the same root as *dayn*, and, while translated as religion, has the connotation of transacting, of repaying the debt that one owes to the Creator, or indeed, to oneself). Madinah is wherever there is a collection of people who pay the debt towards themselves and their Creator in order to be released from the burdens they have accumulated by imitating the misguided ways of their forefathers.

> Surely We have shown him the way: he may be thankful or unthankful. (al-Insan:3)

The *sabil* (way) is the way of *tawhid*. The way of *tawhid*, the way of the mercy of Allah, is already imposed upon all of His creation. Elsewhere the Qur'an says: *kataba `ala nafsihi-r-rahmah*; "He has ordained mercy on Himself" (*al-An`am*:12). Mercy is His overwhelming attribute. Allah possesses everything and everything is under His control and mercy. Allah says that He has shown us the way and the way is through Him. There is only Him – *la ilaha illa-llah*. One is either going to be in a state of gratitude – and when one is grateful his heart is open, tranquil and content and therefore he can see the unity between cause and effect which puts him more in *shukr* (gratitude) – or one is in *kufr* (denial) and will only see aspects of discord.

The way has been imposed on us whether we like it or not. We are all on the way from God to God. We can either recognize the laws of Allah and be grateful to that perfection – and therefore have an easy passage – or disobey them and become injured from constantly hitting the barriers on each side of the road. We are pushed from the experience of the womb to the experience of the tomb, whether we like it or not. The outward, existential passage is the clearly defined way, and the inward *sabil* is the path of abandonment and recognition of *tawhid* and Islam (submission).

We have no control over being born or dying, so what is this arrogance we have meanwhile that makes us think we have any control? The only thing we have control over is the choice of either obeying or disobeying. Obeying the laws brings us into the state of harmony and recognition of the *jannah* (garden). In the Qur'an, the people who have gone to the garden in the next life say that they remember this because they tasted this state before. To have truly tasted it in this life they must have attained a state of true unquestioning abandonment and submission, where the gross and the subtle emerge – that is the true worship.

What we know from the Qur'an about the creation of the physical world and the development of man is closely paralleled by what we have recently come to uncover and discover. Great emphasis is placed upon the cyclical nature of creation. We are given further indications of this by the form of life that exists in the next life. There the solid mass of our bodies, which in this life contains the subtle form of our souls, will appear like a mirage, and what was hidden or secret in our hearts will be clearly manifest. We are told that in the next experience we will be reconstructed according to what we know now in this life, and the knowledge that we can have now is our clarity of mind, purity of heart, and unity between our actions and intentions.

Chapter 3: Growth and Sustenance

Life and growth are inseparable. All physical realities are in dynamic flux and all sentient systems – plants and animals – go through a cycle of growth, maturity, and decline.

Man grows in size and strength physically and usually materially, intellectually, and spiritually. Physical growth generally precedes the other aspects of growth. The gross seems to outdistance the subtle but, in fact, heralds it. Man has no choice in achieving physical growth and equilibrium, for he is driven by basic motives to achieve it, such as hunger, thirst, the need to care for his body, avoidance of pain, and so on.

Growth in knowledge is spurred on by unsatisfactory interaction with the environment and transgression of the bounds. Man soon learns not to question gravitational or, indeed, any other natural physical force. He learns how to enhance physical realities by applying his genius in selective interactions. In chemistry he can bring about new situations by bringing together certain amounts of materials, sometimes in certain manners that do not commonly exist in nature. The same thing applies to all other sciences.

Man differs from all other animals in that he is driven, from birth to death, to use his mind for both physical and spiritual purposes. He is the only animal who has no natural body protection. Nature stripped him of that advantage to enhance a much greater facility, his intellect. Science was born when man began understanding the relationship between cause and effect.

Soon after the physical parts are brought under reasonable balance, man's intellectual and spiritual capacities begin to grow and demand satisfaction. Questions arise: what is the purpose of creation, its beginning and end? Reflection upon these higher meanings is the beginning of man's spiritual growth.

> Allah is He Who created the heavens and the earth and sent down water from the clouds, and brought forth with it fruits as a sustenance for you, and He has made the ships subservient to you, that they might run their course in the sea by His command, and He has made the rivers subservient to you.
>
> And He has made subservient to you the sun and the moon pursuing their courses, and He has made subservient to you the night and the day.
> (Ibrahim:32-33)

For the subtle and timeless to be manifest, it has to be captured in a form that exists within time. Everything to be found in creation – water, vegetation – has been made available to man, and from it he can derive physical sustenance. Even the seas and rivers have been tamed so that he can roam the earth with ease. The sun and the moon, which influence life on earth so much, have also been made for him. From their interaction with earth, we have both night and day and consequently the cycles of rest and work. All of these natural systems of physical phenomena have been created to enable the human system to come into existence, to survive, and to reach its full potential.

The hidden and unknown blessings include all those factors that keep this creation stable and in balance. They are the intangible forces that hold the fabric of this existence together and enable us to be still and reflect.

CHAPTER 3: GROWTH AND SUSTENANCE

> Surely We have made whatever is on the earth an embellishment for it, so that We may try them (as to) which of them is best in works. (al-Kahf:7)

Just as all this sustenance, maintenance, and provision are there for our benefit, so are they a test for us to see whether we get carried away and take them as ends in themselves. They are there to try us and trip us up, not in a bad sense, but only for our growth, just as taking a child on a hike hardens and toughens him up. But when ensuring enough provision for oneself becomes an end in itself, a self-feeding, corrupting cycle of decadence sets in.

Elsewhere the Qur'an says that a culture or community is destroyed by people who are *mutrafun* (plural of *mutraf*, one who lives in sumptuous, excessive luxury and ease), who go for the excesses and become corrupt because of indulging in excessive luxury. The same thing can be a boon as well as a doom. Everything in creation has a positive and a negative application. The Qur'an makes this clear, for it is a complete book.

> God is He Who made subservient to you the sea that the ships may run therein by His command, and that you may seek of His grace, and that you may give thanks. (al-Jathiyah:12)

Man will reflect upon this short experience of life only when he is in a neutral and reflective state, and that usually comes about when he is content and in gratitude. When one is clothed, fed, and sheltered from the elements, one is at least physically protected from the harsh and distracting pursuits for one's basic needs, and can be, for a moment, grateful. In that state of gratitude one's heart is open, soft, receptive, and free from concern.

The experience of this life is for the heart to be in that state, for it to reflect the divine story, the divine purpose of life. The heart is like a pond of water; it reflects well if it is still, badly if it is agitated. Its capacity for clear reflection is as good as its calmness and contentment. *Shukr* (gratitude) is what is intended by all these provisions and the knowledge that comes with them.

The Qur'an says: *La`in shakartum la-azidannakum*; "if you are grateful, I would certainly give to you more" (*Ibrahim*:7). The more one is grateful, the more God will increase one in that knowledge until he reaches a point of absolute certainty that he is not an animal who has come here only to die.

The Qur'an promises that this life is only an experience, a test for man to grow and be readied for another state about which he can only have a description in an allegorical form. This is the ultimate *rizq* (provision) or sustenance.

On the physical side of sustenance, the Qur'an tells us of so many communities that had a great deal of prosperity and well-being, but because of their transgression and deviation from the natural path of the divine laws, they were doomed. The people of Moses, 'Ād, Hud, Lot and others, were those who transgressed. They were warned, told why, and were shown the way, but they became arrogant and they, like all other such cultures, collapsed. Frequently, it was natural phenomena that brought about their ruin. The Qur'an tells us to visit the sites of their cities and see what happened. Like the people of Salih in north-eastern Arabia, they built well and had so much. All that is left now are the ruins of those palaces that had been carved into the hills.

Elsewhere the Qur'an says: *Wa ma zalamnahum wa lakin kanu anfusahum yazlimun*; "and We did them no injustice, but they were unjust to themselves" (*an-Nahl*:118). Justice takes place on this earth by bringing to an end those who have not evolved enough to recognize the divine laws; they will be doomed on this earth.

Anna-l-arda yarithuha `ibadiya-s-salihun; "(as for) the land, My righteous servants shall inherit it" (*al-Anbiya'*:105). "Righteous servants" means those who are evolved, those who know what is right and wrong, those who recognize, differentiate, and act accordingly, not those who just recognize and then do nothing about it. The Qur'an is very clear about this point.

There will be a time on this earth when there will be highly evolved spiritual beings. From the Qur'anic point of view, there is evolutionary progress. Man begins as a clot in the womb and grows into a fully fledged being; creation was a dense dot and then expanded explosively into our universe. Man reaches his highest point in a global sense when the *Mahdi* (literally, the rightly guided one) appears. The Qur'an gives us the background and backbone, and the rest of it we learn from the Prophet, *salla-llahu `alayhi wa alihi wa sallam*. That last stage of existence on this earth, in which man will be fully evolved, will begin after the appearance of the *Mahdi* when justice will prevail. According to the traditions, this stage will last for some time; it will not be for just one or two days. Therefore we believe that the world will not come to an end, even if great wars and destruction occur.

> And one of His signs is that He created mates for you from yourselves that you may find rest in them, and He put between you love and compassion; most surely there are signs in this for a people who reflect. (ar-Rum: 21)

Mankind is created from one self; and the meaning of the higher self is higher consciousness. We are all conscious of the attributes of creation that we experience. On the physical level we are conscious of cold and heat, health and illness, sleep and wakefulness, emptiness, and fullness. We are also conscious of feelings such as love and hate, peace and agitation, anger, and contentment. Where we differ among ourselves is in what causes these feelings or attributes in us, the extent of their manifestation, and the result of the direction to which they are aimed. Being angry can drive one person to violence, another to a long-term plan, another to immediate corrective action, and yet another to patience, perseverance and gentle reaction. Yet, we all come from one self.

In this existence, which is balanced on the forces of opposites, the highest creation in it – the human creation – is also balanced on the opposites of man and woman. In every man there is a woman, and in every woman there is a man. If the two meet on the physical and outer level, then a taste of that oneness, that unified wholeness, is experienced. *Sakana* is to dwell in, to be peaceful, quiet. Potentially, this pairing of man and woman can achieve that.

"And He put between you love and compassion." Because man and woman are so similar and yet appear to have dissimilarities, especially on the physical level, a certain affinity between the two is brought about. It is part of the overall affinity towards unification. In the duality that is driving and enabling us to achieve a measure of unification, there is a great sign, a signpost along the path of *tawhid*, telling us the direction of the path of *tawhid*. The fact that man and woman find a certain measure of unity, and an affinity towards that unity, is a proof that everything in this existence points to that direction, to that ultimate end of full realization of the oneness in this existence.

> Glory to Him Who created pairs of all things, of what the earth grows, and of their kind and of what they do not know. (Ya Sin: 36)

Once a person has realized the immense fact that life is experienced along the polarity of opposites and that man's consciousness drives him to see the unifying principle – or the

CHAPTER 3: GROWTH AND SUSTENANCE

subtle force or point – in which all these opposites are united, both in their origin and in their destiny, there emerges great wisdom and recognition of the one net which encompasses the entire balance of life. With this wisdom comes the natural exclamation of exaltation and glorification of the obvious puzzle of everything being cast as an aspect of duality – man/woman, good/bad, living/dead, and so on. Yet, each aspect is only a branch that stems from one root; and the two branches announce the fact that they have one common origin by joining together at the tree's trunk.

> Most surely in the variation of the night and the day, and what Allah has created in the heavens and the earth, there are signs for a people who guard (against evil). (Yunus:6)

Taqwa (fearful awareness, related to *yattaqun*) is the process of recognition, avoidance and prevention of undesirables. It is fearful awareness of being in a state that is not conducive to well-being. Man's drive towards harmony, peace, and the appropriate relationship with his environment becomes efficient and achieves its end when the boundaries are delineated. One will move along the highway more efficiently when he knows where the edges are, and so the edges are starkly marked, with cats' eyes or with barriers. Once one knows the boundaries, consciously or unconsciously, the chances are that he will keep to the middle of the road. The middle of the road is the recognition that its two sides are the extremes, the polarities. If one's consciousness and his awareness place him in the middle, then whenever he is conscious of any of the edges, he realizes that they are there simply to guide him rather than to trip him.

The opposites of day and night, light and darkness, activity and rest show that life is based on opposites, and man contains the meaning of both the extremes. One of them is still and almost timeless, and the other is experiencing the agitation of time. Man is both: he contains the experience and the recognition of time, as well as the secret of eternal time – non-time, absolute silence. In reflecting upon that, in recognizing that we are held within vast bounds – at one extreme timelessness, and at the other the immensely speedy passage of time – man becomes conscious of the vastness of his potential in this existence.

> Do you not see that Allah has made what is in the heavens and what is in the earth subservient to you, and made complete to you His favors outwardly and inwardly? And among men is he who disputes regarding Allah though having no knowledge, nor guidance, nor a book giving light. (Luqman:20)

Men of reflection will come to realize the uniquely high station that has been bestowed upon man through their intellect and consciousness. Whatever he can conceive of and perceive in the heavens and earth, he realizes its use and its part in this unified field of existence. Whenever a man is aware of a phenomenon, he sees its role and its importance in this jigsaw puzzle, in the interconnectedness of creation. All of the creational elements, visible or invisible, discernible or indiscernible, having been discovered or not, are there as a platform and backdrop to man's consciousness.

One can therefore say that all creation in both the heavens and earth is for man's benefit, at the limited physical level for a better quality of life and at the spiritual level for contemplation and realization of the one and only creational force. If man does not discover the realities in the heavens and earth along this direction, he will only come up with theories and assumptions which no doubt will prove to be false. In other words, whatever he discovered will make sense and will have meaning if it is understood as part of *tawhid* (divine unity). If he does not apply long-term vision and cannot place his discoveries within the totality of creation, the cosmos will appear to be chaos. For example, upon seeing a very slow-moving car swerving to the right, he may conclude that it is going to make a right turn, and yet it is only veering to the right in order to take a left turn. If had viewed the journey in its totality, he would have seen that the movement to the right was really to facilitate its movement to the left.

Often our theories and observations in this life are short-term in the sense of creational time and therefore we are misled. If we always bear in mind the assumption of complete mercy and *tawhid* and understand that everyone has been created in order to recognize his Creator, then those short-term mistakes will be regarded as positive lessons.

> And He made subservient to you whatsoever is in the heavens and whatever is in the earth, all, from Himself; most surely there are signs in this for a people who reflect. (al-Jathiyah:13)

This *ayah* reconfirms that everything in existence is for man's benefit, and it also implies that man's consciousness, if it is pure, can encompass all creational beings. In other words, we will gain access one way or another to the knowledge of everything in creation if we are in *tafakkur*, which is pure reflection or meditation. Reflection is not pure if it has a purpose. If it is not a natural part of submission and if it does not come as a gift of that submission, if it is directed by us, we will only be restricting the field of vision. Whatever is in the heavens and earth exists in order to facilitate and enable us to grow further and mature as spiritual beings.

> And He has made subservient for you the night and the day and the sun and the moon, and the stars are made subservient by His command; most surely there are signs in this for a people who ponder. (an-Nahl:12)

Man is driven to develop his `aql, his faculty of cognizance, reasoning, and understanding. Understanding implies an ever widening field of vision. The more man broadens his field of vision, the more accurate becomes his understanding. If his field of vision is wider in respect to time, his understanding will be accurate and usable at all times. If it is wider geographically, then his understanding of his observations will apply to a broader ecological setting.

Day and night, which encompass us, are the two extremes of experiential realities within us – dynamism and stillness, light and darkness, the sun and the moon. The stars are manifestations that beam and transmit the light of the unfolding network that has emerged from the command to create. They all unfold according to the decree of the order of the Creator along a scientifically and fully prescribed path. By contemplating these elements that are essential parts of the foundation of existence, our faculty of reason will be expanded. The more we reflect upon these opposites and the situations that we are in, the more our faculty of reasoning will widen and the horizons of our knowledge broaden.

These *ayat* (communications; signs; verses), as well as many others, clearly indicate man's chosen position in creation. Earthly creation is part of the Creator's mercy for man to choose, by himself, with his own intellectual awakening and discrimination, the correct path of action so that he may taste and gain the knowledge of the fire and the garden here. It is the ultimate mercy of the Creator to give His creation this paramount responsibility of choice – the freedom to choose with the understanding and knowledge that come from trial and error and the experimentation he undertakes during his lifetime. Sustenance is there for him to go through the cycles of obedience and disobedience, certainty and doubt, in order for him to be experientially confirmed as well as inwardly certain that there is One Creator behind all this existence and that what appears to be diverse and opposite in this existence actually emanates from one source. If he abandons himself into that source, he will discover and experience the ultimate form of sustenance. If he truly and knowledgeably submits to it, then his existence will become fully meaningful; it will be a conscious preparation for its purpose: to enter the timeless eternal zone.

Chapter 4: The Meaning of Time

Man as a biological and physical entity is conceived, is born, lives, and dies in the dimension of time. While he exists, he also personally experiences the relativity of time. Certain events seem to last much longer than others; unpleasant moments linger longer than pleasant ones: a relaxing vacation passes very quickly, but a prison sentence takes ages. Living with people one likes is very easy; a year can pass without notice. If one keeps the company of disagreeable people, he counts every minute. Understanding this relativity of time implies that within man there is a built-in gauge that measures this changeable thing called time.

If we believe in the message of the Qur'an that man is basically a divine creature and that God is closer to him than his jugular vein, we will see that the main attribute of God is His timelessness. All the changes and fluctuations of this process called time are reflected upon an unchanging motionless, timeless dimension within man.

The Creator is in non-time; from Him comes time. The created being lives in time, experiences in time, and somehow the timeless dimension to which he will ultimately return is echoed within him. He has come from that zone of pre-creation and will return to that eternity. If he is returned to that eternity properly equipped, that is, conscious and awakened, then he will experience the state of the garden. If he is not properly equipped, then he will experience the recycling in the fire. Allah is in "non-time", man is in time; but Allah pervades all, permeates all, contains all; therefore man can gain understanding as well as insights and openings into non-time.

If one stretches time into millions and millions of units and then stretches those units into infinity, he will reach a point of "non-time". Infinity has the same qualities as zero. If one takes something to its limit, it will turn into its opposite. Take an hour and make it into a day, a month, a year, make it thousands of years, make it light years, extend it to its boundaries, and it will collapse into a non-time zone, into zero time. The Qur'an alludes to this in many verses. A saying in Arabic says: *Kulla shay`in ta`adda haddah inqalaba ila diddah*, "Anything that goes to its limit will revert into its opposite." In this existence, time is relative, and the Qur'an reflects this clearly.

> To Him ascend the angels and the spirit in a day the measure of which is fifty thousand years. (al-Ma`arij:4)

Here the final day is implied, the day of reckoning, when everything is beyond time. On that day the angels and the spirit (the higher spirit, the *ruh*) return to God, because that day is the day of return. Everything will gather and return to the single Entity, to that single point. They will all ascend on that day, the measure of which is fifty thousand years. In other words, the measures of time we use here are only measures of technological convenience.

That day will unwind so slowly for us that we will be able to witness ourselves in slow motion, which can be the greatest agony and the greatest purification for many of us. At the end of that day, we may acknowledge that we have had enough of agony, and from then on we may witness the mercy of Allah.

This *ayah* shows us the final day as we may experience it, as thousands of years. One interpretation of this *ayah* is that life as man knows it will last fifty thousand years, and the Final Day will balance that out with the same amount of time. There are still other interpretations. What is generally agreed on is that the word *yawm* (day) in the Qur'an is used to indicate a period of time and not necessarily twenty-four hours.

> Therefore endure with a goodly patience. (al-Ma`arij:5)

This is an injunction to the Prophet, peace and blessings be upon him, and to us. If man finds that whatever he is doing is to no avail, he must be patient. Patience means biding time. If he has patience with something, then he will reduce the period of endurance to zero-time.

> Surely they think it to be far off, and We see it nigh. (al-Ma`arij:6-7)

They see the end of the world as being far away in time; but the truth, from beyond time, says "We see it nigh!" For people of learning the end is most urgent. If one truly makes his own reckoning now, he will bring on a state in himself similar to that on the day of reckoning. It is for this reason that many people, even semi-spiritual ones, say that one should make a reckoning at the end of each day, that is, settle one's accounts. Each of us should find out what we have done and why we have done it. We should not postpone things or brush them underneath the carpet. If we are willing to face up to all our accounts every minute of the day, they we will be up-to-date. We can see the end as being near, and yet for us time does not exist. Biologically, we are moving in time, yet we have a timeless consciousness. We will have already entered that state which we will experience anyway.

> And they ask you to hasten on the punishment,
> and God will by no means fail in His promise, and
> surely a day with your Lord is as a thousand years
> of what you number. (al-Hajj:47)

A day from the viewpoint of Him Who is beyond time can be any amount of time by our measurement, fifty thousand years, a thousand years, or one day, because from the timeless point of view there is no time. We, on the other hand, are at the other end of the spectrum. The closer we get to God the shorter the time. At a certain point, it may be a thousand years. When closer to God it may be an instant; and then, not even that.

Another reference in the Qur'an to the relativity of time is in *surat al-Qadr*. "The night of power is better than a thousand months" (*al-Qadr*:3). *Laylat ul-qadr* (the night of power) is the night of knowledge of the measure, of the knowledge of the Book – the night that the Qur'an descended. It is the night in which you wake up to confront your knowledge, the night in which you become awake and know that there is only Allah. The final book (the Qur'an) descended in its totality on *laylat ul-qadr*, and it took years to completely unfold from the heart of the Prophet, peace and blessings be upon him.

The essential meaning of *laylat ul-qadr* must also have an actual physical form. There cannot be a form without a meaning or a meaning without a form, a cause without an effect or an effect without a cause. The night in which knowledge in its final form came to the world – through the light of that perfect mirror, the Prophet Muhammad, peace and blessings be upon him – is better than a thousand months, that is, better than all the months. Look at the actualization of its meaning: there were a thousand months of the darkness of the Umayyad rule. It was for that period of time exactly that they governed and tried to make Islam into yet another religion to be used for wielding power and exercising control, rather than its being a *din*, a spiritually based code of conduct; for the way to a man's freedom is through the containment of his outer behavior.

In every year there is only one night in which the course of events becomes clear and it is the night of power, clarity and knowledge, the night in which the light of reality shines most. The Qur'an and traditions indicate that it is one of the nights during the last ten days of Ramadan (the month of fasting). During such a radiant night and such easy circumstances, the meditating worshipper will find it easier to attune to the nature of reality and the divine laws and thereby adjust his desires, will, and expectations more appropriately to the limiting factors that are imposed upon him. It can be the night that the individual's tuning fork is in harmony with the creational orchestra.

If there is complete and utter harmony between the individual and his environment, the individual will experience acceptance with knowledge. Gratitude emerging from that knowledge will in turn lead to bliss. At that point, time becomes almost irrelevant. If one is truly and fully drunk without the biological side-effects time almost ceases for him, and that is the state most of us seek. We naturally get bored or dislike time that goes by slowly in order to find a way into that timeless state of which we occasionally catch a glimpse when our desires and expectations are fully met for a moment. If we can attain that balance at all times, then time becomes meaningless.

The awakened sleeper cannot but be alert and aware. Once he has fully awakened to the purpose and direction of life, the meaning of biological time will be much modified. His perspective of it will be forever changed. The nature of man is such that his essence or origin arises from non-time. His *ruh* is so subtle and divine and yet he can experience physical reality in this life, with its physical, chemical and biological limitations. He has emerged from non-time into time and will return to infinite time. While in the prison of time he longs for the state of non-time. In fact, the experiencing of time in all its ranging relationships can only be supported on a foundation which is absolute – "non-time" belongs to the Originator of this creation.

Chapter 5: Grinding to a Halt

Any beginning has an end, and yet, because of a strange veil of heedlessness that man tends to pull over himself, we find that he does not visualize or think about his own end. If his end were in sight, it is most likely that he would use the time leading up to it fully, efficiently and with a sense of urgency. Man is a thinking animal. He is driven to use his faculty of thought by his need to meet his daily physical requirements. Throughout his life he thinks about, plans, and reviews his existential well-being. It would be a natural conclusion for him to also think about the end of his journey through life.

> A questioner asked about the chastisement which must befall the unbelievers – there is none to avert it. From God, the word of the ways of Ascent. (al-Ma'arij:1-3)

Surat al-Ma`arij* begins with the doubting questioner wanting to know what the end will be like. *Ma`arij (ways of ascent) is from *`araja*, to ascend, mount, or limp. The fall of Adam is his ascension. He was brought into this world in order to ascend. Man's own ascension lies in his recognition and awareness of what causes him to fall, and that is based on choice. A fully programmed, pulsating being has no choice; his actions are predictable. Flexibility and choice mark the rise of intelligence. The maturation of intelligence comes about when the right choice is made.

With this flexibility and choice comes discrimination. The healthy, intelligent person internalizes the teachings of old experiences and continues to learn from new ones. Wisdom is the inner program according to which a person with wide experience acts. The more encompassing that wisdom is, the more harmonious and successful is the action. Ultimately, when wisdom and intelligence are optimal, choice and flexibility are minimal. If one is able to bring into the formula all the relevant factors pertaining to a situation at hand, the best course of action will be a specifically defined one – no choice. Man therefore goes through a full cycle that starts with no choice and ends with no choice, but the last phase is confirmed by his faculty of reason.

> Do they not reflect within themselves: Allah did not create the heavens and earth and what is between them but with truth, and (for) an appointed term? And most surely most of the people are deniers of the meeting of their Lord. (ar-Rum:8)

God created the heavens and the earth and that no man's land between them with truth, that is, with absolute knowledge and justice. This creation has a limited existence; it will not last forever. Most people avoid the fact that they will eventually meet their Lord.

It is love and attachment to this world that makes us forget that we will return back to our source, our Sustainer, our Lord, the Creator, the Everlasting. The hurly-burly of the outer world and the physical aspects of life make us forget and cause us to lapse into *ghaflah*, heedlessness, carelessness, and neglect; and these are the attributes of *Shaytan*. *Shaytan* is what makes us neglectful or fearful of provision. That element within us makes us negative and niggardly.

CHAPTER 5: GRINDING TO A HALT

> And one of His signs is your sleeping and your seeking of His bounty, by night and (by) day. Surely there are signs in this for a people who would hear. (ar-Rum:23)

The common courtesy towards the night is to sleep, that is, to let our outer form rest. If one wants to awaken his inner core, however, it is better to do so during the night when all the distractions of the day are at a minimum. When one wants to see the birth of night, he watches the sunset. If one wants to awaken his innermost self, he has to wait until his outermost self is asleep and deadened to the world. If he wants to see Allah, he must experience death. If he wants only to see Allah he becomes dead to other than Allah.

Nahar, day, implies toil and outer growth. Man cannot have outer growth without inner growth. He cannot claim that he is a man of the inner life and abuse everybody else outwardly. If a man says he is a sufi but wreaks havoc in the land, he is living a contradiction, a lie. If he is a sufi, he should follow the meaning of the three letters of its root word *suf: sad, waw,* and *fe*. Imam 'Ali, upon him be peace, said *sad* stands for *sidq* (sincerity) and *safa* (purity); *waw* stands for *widd* (love) and *wafa* (faithfulness); and *fe* stands for *faqr* (poverty) and *fana* (self-obliteration). If one stands for these, the outer is unified with the inner and the inner with the outer. Otherwise, he will at best limp through life. Ultimately, the only person who suffers from these lies is the individual.

There are signs for people who are receptive to them, who hear and heed the warning signals. Hearing is the first sense we experience when we are born. Even in the womb a child can hear the name of Allah in the beat of the mother's heart – Allah, Allah, Allah.

> And one of His signs is that He shows you the lightning for fear and for hope, and sends down water from the clouds, then gives life therewith to the earth after its death; most surely there are signs in this for a people who understand (ar-Rum:24)

If there is a great deal of fear of seeing these phenomena, we have to express it outwardly because we are unifiers of the outward and the inward. A Muslim expresses this truth by performing special prayers. Whenever a significant disturbance occurs, be it a natural phenomenon such as an eclipse or a sudden fearful turbulence in the heart, this prayer simply acknowledges his need of his Lord. It is a proof of his submission. It is not performed in order to beseech God to stop these phenomena. What is decreed will happen.

> And every soul shall be paid back fully (for) what it has done, and He knows best what they do. (az-Zumar:70)

Every soul will be repaid. The individual is the author of his own illusions and the doer of his own actions. Man is given this long lifetime so that he can reconstruct the Truth within himself. It is the divine One who is within you, the sublime One, the abandoned One, the free One, the one and only One – Allah within you. He is the absolute Knower of what has been done, of what is being done, and what will be done.

> But when the deafening cry comes, ('Abasa:33)

This *ayah* describes one of the first conditions of the last day, of reckoning. *As-sakhkhah* is the final call. It is what closes off the hearing so that nothing makes sense any more. The deafening cry heralds the end to the systems of perception and comprehension as we understand them. It is sound that drowns out all other sounds, like the blasts of a trumpet. The forceful wind expanding through a narrow passageway shoutingly announces the blowing away of the earth's solidity.

> The day on which a man shall flee from his brother, And his mother and his father, and his wife and his children ('Abasa:34-6)

When that day comes, man's condition will be one of intense disorientation, as if he has run away from the brother he loves, who is like him and has helped him, who has given him a reason to exist by serving and helping.

When the physical foundation for existential stability disintegrates, all other forces, powers and links that maintained the harmony and equilibrium of life on earth will collapse. All relationships will disintegrate. A brother will not recognize a brother, and every self will be centered on itself. The urgency and disruption of that time is beyond our normal comprehension. In circumstances when mother nature is no longer reliable, man will also flee from his biological mother. The security of any past established relationship is rendered meaningless in the face of mass upheaval and cacophony.

> Every man of them shall on that day have an affair which will occupy him. (`Abasa:37)

The day of reckoning is a great shock because it is the beginning of a new life, a new experience. All the dead will be resurrected, everything will become clear and exposed, and all the little things that we considered insignificant are clearly magnified and revealed to be important. The consequences of all the things we have done in this existence, which we thought could be forgotten about or were of no consequence, will be exposed. We will clearly see in a subtle form all the people in this life who reminded us of God and the next life but whom we dismissed. All the accounts that we have not settled in this world, all our lack of awareness, all our hypocrisies, all those years of only having concerned ourselves with our material existence, all the different idols we worshipped and the different excuses we gave – they will all instantly appear before us.

As a result of these events there will be major havoc. Everybody will be concerned about himself. Nobody will be able to remember his offspring or his mother, father, wife or wealth; everyone will be concerned about his own state and situation. The end will be so sharp and decisive that there will be no possibility of any crutches or aids – each will be on his own.

> (Many) faces on that day shall be bright, laughing, joyous. ('Abasa:38-9)

The face of the one who is in *tawhid*, who has unified himself with destiny – who has abandoned himself to Allah, lived for Allah, and is returned to Allah – will on that day be distinguished by its bright and unveiled light. *Musfirah* (shining bright) means that their abandonment is clear on their faces. The verbal root of *musfirah* means to unveil, reveal, expose, and travel. When one travels, he is exposed and vulnerable; he reveals himself to the rest of the world. The man of *tawhid* will joyously reflect his reality because he has lived with the certainty of Truth.

> And (many) faces on that day, on them shall be dust, darkness shall cover them: These are they who deny the truth, the iniquitous. ('Abasa:40-42)

Other faces on that day will be covered with dust. They will not yet have shaken the dust of their *nafs* (lower self) off their souls. They will still be tarnished with the dust of what they have inscribed on their hearts. On this day they will be unable to sing the song of Truth or even to reflect it.

The purpose of this existence is for us to stop singing our own songs so that the one and only song bubbles up through our hearts. But as we know, we constantly play our own compositions. Those on the dark side of denial shall be covered with dust, exhausted. This occurrence implies that the gold within them – their reality – has not been mined. They have not seen their true reality because they have allowed dust to settle thickly over it. Tired with the weight of the dust, they are the unbelievers who wreaked havoc on this earth.

> And on the day that the enemies of God shall be brought together to the fire, then they shall be formed into groups. Until when they come to it, their ears and their eyes and their skins shall bear witness against them as to what they did. (Ha Mim:19-20)

Hashara is to gather, to come together. The whole of creation was originally gathered together. Then the heavens and the earth were split. In the end everything will once again be gathered. The creational reality will collapse and come to its final resting place. It will revert into that unfathomable dense matter it once was.

Man has always sought to discover the fundamental particle of matter in this creation. Scientists try to measure and create mathematical equations about it. Contemporary scientists illustrate the density of the primal matter by saying that if one were to put it in a thimble it would weigh billions of tons. The density is so great that we can no longer conceive of it. It is not even a dot. It is the command "Be", and it is. The physical creation will collapse back into that denseness and beyond intellectual comprehension. Its energy, or its echo, is the gathering that is described.

Men are not just physical entities; they also have souls or spirits. On that day those electromagnetic bundles which are called souls will all be joined. All souls emanate from one source, like sparks flying out of a fire, reaching a certain height (age) and returning after having been processed or oxidized.

Once the gatheredness has occurred, everything will be sorted out according to its quality. The screening and segregating process is totally just. Those who are fit for a final, unending, bottomless pit will be in the fire of *jahannam* (hell). Their ears, eyes, and skins will give witness against them. At that time they are whatever they have heard, seen, or felt. There can be no separation from what is absorbed through experience, and there certainly is no running away from it. For this reason, the Prophet, peace and blessings be upon him, would not hear anything bad about anyone. He would say that this sort of poison was more difficult for him to clean out than food poisoning. With the latter one vomits, but after a day or so he recovers. But the poison which you have heard about someone you love or trust is going to take longer to get rid of. One should therefore cover his ears because he wants to safeguard himself. His ear will give witness to what it has heard. Man is what he hears and sees.

"Their skins shall bear witness" means that every individual's story is genetically encoded in his chromosomes, within the DNA of every cell. Every cell contains the entire story of one's physical strengths and weaknesses, of what he has gathered, and of what he is. One cannot be divided into separate parts, for he is one total entity. Each one of us is the product of past actions and thoughts combined, superimposed on the actions, thoughts, and environment of everything around us. I am the result of my past. The future is where my will now takes me, superimposing upon and interacting with the will and destiny of everyone else. If I am a spiritual seeker and want to make my quest easier, I would keep the company of seekers. Otherwise, I would have to single-handedly overcome the ill of millions of people who are against truth.

Witnessing one's actions will take place without being able to do anything about them. All his life man has hushed up this witnessing in the court of the *nafs* (lower self) within him. Every time that goodness wants to stand up and show those actions and intentions in a true light, he shuts it up. The corridors of his *nafs* do not allow his own witnesser to come out. But, in reality, there is no *nafs*. There is only the *nafs al-wahidah*, the One Self – God – Who is in charge.

> And they shall say to their skins: Why have you borne witness against us? They shall say: God who makes everything speak has made us speak, and He created you at first, and to Him you shall be brought back. (Ha Mim:21)

It is God Who makes everything sing its song. He makes us speak our truth. We are all slaves of truth. God made every part of everything reflect its reality. Each aspect, right down to the skin, the cells, the genetic codes, is made to sing its song. We do not hear it because we are so deaf. We cannot even look at our own actions of yesterday in an impartial light. We deny our responsibility; we say that something else got into us when we did such and such – we were not ourselves. But if it was not us, then who was it?

A great shaykh once said to me: "I'll tell you one thing, Allah is easy. It is man who is most difficult. Stop the man, and Allah is

Allah", that is, stop the "you", the "I", put *shaytan* in a cage, and melt the key in love for God so that there is no possibility of it being reopened. This is the best action one can take. Otherwise, as it is with most of us, we will find that the key always reappears and we become like maniacs running around the countryside trying to catch the animal that has run out of the zoo, the zoo of our *nafs*. Melt the key to the cage in the Qur'anic truth and your *shaytan* will submit; as the Prophet, peace and blessings be upon him, said: "My *shaytan* has given up, it has submitted, it is in Islam."

> And you did not veil yourselves lest your ears and your eyes and your skins should bear witness against you, but you thought that Allah did not know most of what you did. (Ha Mim:22)

Man cannot stop his ears, eyes, and skin witnessing against him. He cannot stop the *sunnah* of Allah. He cannot alter the decree of perfection. He has wrongly imagined that God does not know what he does. He thought that he could cover up his actions because inwardly he was in such an isolated state. He was not in *tawhid*. When he attains the *maqam al-ihsan*, the highest state of correct action and behavior, he behaves as though God sees him in every second, even though he does not see Him. He will act as if there is a video camera recording his inner intentions and outer actions at all times and at any moment it can freeze.

The meaning of *dhikr* is awareness, or remembrance. If one can suddenly picture oneself in a moment of anger – his hand raised to hit a child because he took his biscuit – if he can freeze that frame, he will not be likely to do it again or at least, the chances of it recurring are less. If one makes every moment his day of resurrection – the day that man must reckon with himself, his *nafs*, and is ashamed of his vulgarity, madness, stupidity and arrogance – these unhealthy, destructive traits will disappear.

> And that was your (evil) thought which you entertained about your Lord that has tumbled you down into perdition, thus you have become one of the lost ones. (Ha Mim:23)

Man's madness, his evil thoughts and doubts, made him stumble and tumble down into those same conditions of his first life. His next life will echo this life. All these things were real: they were witnessed, they were seen. My ears heard, my eyes saw, and my hand did; but I did not really know where I was. Then where was I? The answer of the Qur'an is: in *ghaflah*, heedlessness, but we call it bad luck. A man walks across the street, but because he is distracted by the perfume of a woman, or of anything that represents the lower self, he is looking in only one direction. He then stumbles on a stone, he is run over by a taxi, and for six months he is incapacitated; and we call it "bad luck". It was no such thing; he was in *ghaflah*.

Such is the state of the people who are at a loss. The people of *jahannam* (hell) are told: You doubted and you got lost; you lost. You did not have *iman* (faith). Everything hinges on *iman*. If one has *iman*, that is enough. Those at a loss do not understand that the *Rabb*, the Sustainer, the Lord is in control.

> Then if they will endure, the fire is still their abode, and if they ask for goodwill, then they are not of those who shall be granted goodwill.
>
> And we have appointed for them intimate companions so they have made fair-seeming to them what is before them and what is behind them, and the word proved true against them – among the nations of the jinn and the men that

> have passed away before them – that they shall
> surely be losers. (Ha Mim:24-25)

Those who remain in that state, in that interspace between the first blow and the second blow until the end, will only experience burning agony. They are in turmoil and apprehension. Their patience will only bring fire. This *ayah* is very applicable to us nowadays. Patience is an attribute of Allah – *as-Sabur* (the Everpatient). But patience with injustice and wrong action is a door to the fire.

These people who are at a loss will have their own companions, who are also at a loss. The truth, the word of eternal, absolute Truth, is reflected in them, as it was reflected in people before them. "Before them" refers to events that historically preceded them on this earth, and can also refer to different types of beings. God says that men of wrong action, the dwellers of the fire, will be in the company of those who left the world before and those who may come later, all of these people with a similar destiny. In the state after death, that is, after this world, the grouping or selection will be done according to everyone's condition, not according to the time or place in which they experienced life. As far as God is concerned, then and now are one because God is *al-Da`m* (the Eternal). God is beyond time; He is endless. If one only lives now, if he has no past or future, then he lives on *iman* (faith), and *iman* shows him the meaning of endlessness. It will give him the certainty of the non-ending, eternal realm from which this short period that is life has come.

> And they ask you to hasten on the punishment,
> and God will by no means fail in His promise; and
> surely a day with your Lord is as a thousand years
> of what you number. (al-Hajj:47)

We fail to recognize that we may inadvertently be weaving our own hell through our wrong actions, ignorance, expectations, and attachments, right now in this life.

The final agony of the timeless zone will come on the day when chastisement will cover the deniers of truth. It will overwhelm from above and from beneath their feet. God will say: "Taste what you did." If we are unable to taste the effects of our intentions, that is, the reactions to our actions, now, the Qur'an tells us that in the next life we will certainly do so because that is what we will have become; we will be the taste itself. Therefore, if we are sensitive now we will be in fear. We will know what is going to cause us damage here and now, and that is awareness of transgressing the boundary.

> On that day We will set a seal upon their mouths, and their hands shall speak to Us, and their feet shall bear witness of what they earned. (Ya Sin:65)

Trust and *iman* must be translated into our outer action. Man cannot just have an inner without an outer. He cannot claim that he has good intentions while they do not manifest themselves. From the point of view of the *mu'min* (believer) he has to be in *jihad* (literally, utmost exertion – for the sake of God – and by extension, so-called holy war), not only to realize his inner intentions, but also to fulfill one of the injunctions of *shari`ah* (revealed Islamic code of behavior). If he cannot ward off evil and act upon goodness, the next best thing he can do is act by his tongue. And if he cannot even do that, then his heart should be kept safe by moving, because the cybernetics of what is going on will send those people and that situation to their doom and everything will collapse. He has to be in *jihad*.

Every cell will vibrate, emanate, and transmit its story. Whatever we do, whatever action we take, whatever intention is behind our actions now will be recorded in every cell. Within the DNA molecules the whole story is inscribed anyway. Every cell contains our entire overall make-up, and everything else we are acting upon will be recorded within each cell.

Our feet and hands will also bear witness to what we have earned. The hand here symbolizes the physicalization of intention into action. Through our actions our intentions will be visible and clear. The so-called "you" – the bundle of you which will be brought into the next existence without any possibilities of protection – will sing its song and show its reality. If we are insensitive to the unification between our actions and our intentions day in day out, we will eventually become aware of them on the Day of Judgment. On that day there will be nothing other than clarity because we will be our actions personified.

> And it shall be said: Today We forsake you as you neglected the meeting of this day of yours and your abode is the fire, and there are not for you any helpers: (al-Jathiyah:34)

We will not be neglected because we were in separation. We were not on the path of *tawhid*, we were in *shirk*, (associating other-than-God with God). We were seeing two, "I" and Reality. We were in arrogance, following the path of "I-ness". We were not in abandonment and submission; we were not engulfed by *iman*. We did not allow ourselves to drown in that sea of mercy and trust, from which the unification of action and intention comes. The end of a process no doubt contains the meaning of the entire process. The end is the result of all interactions that have taken place. It is the distillation of multiple elements and forces asserting themselves upon each other along the passage of time. Since man desires stability, predictability, reliability, peace and harmony during his life, he therefore expects and wishes for his end also to be dominated by these qualities. These are descriptions of the state of the garden. The state of the fire is its opposite – ever agitated, neither alive nor dead, perpetually troubled, falling into a bottomless pit. In his life he practices the role that he will experience in the next life. If he plays the predominating role in this life with a sincere, unified and conscious effort along a prescribed path of knowledge, then there is no doubt that his end will also contain and reflect the peace of the garden.

Chapter 6: The Final Collapse

The Qur'an describes the end of this creation as a catastrophic event, a day of great noise or cacophony, when mountains will float away and everything will collapse upon itself. The physicality of creation will disintegrate and vanish into nothingness. The orbital courses of the sun, moon, and stars will be disrupted so that they will all be brought together. The end of the physical expanding universe is the beginning of disintegration and collapse.

> And the mountains shall be moved off so that they shall remain a mere semblance. (an-Naba':20)

The verbal root of *sarab* (semblance, mirage) is to flow or leak, and in one form means to slink away, or to glide along. The closer one gets to the mirage, the more it disappears. The more one tries to find it, to unify with it, the further it is from one. One great master says: *hadhihi-d-dunya sarab*, "(the whole of) this world is a mirage". It will never nourish man. He may think it is all about getting this situation fixed up, this house, that job, this freedom; but when he reaches his goal, he realizes that it is not what he had expected to be.

The mountains will, in time, revert to their original components. They will disintegrate from solid mass into dust, and the dust will become gas, and finally everything will disappear as if one were seeing a film of creation in reverse. The process of creation that first occurred from the explosion of dense matter will be repeated in reverse at the end of time.

We experience an echo of that in our own lifetime, for

after reaching maturity we begin to decline, as though back into childhood. After the cosmos matures, it will also decline; reverting in time, it will become a mirage and recede as it came forth.

> When the sun is covered, And when the stars darken, (at-Takwir:1-2)

The verbal root of the word *kuwwirat* (is covered) is to roll or wrap something up, to make it into a round bundle; from it is derived the word for ball, *kurah*. It indicates that the sun is no longer a spherical expanse, bubbling with explosions, but will collapse upon and consume itself.

Kadura, the root of *inkadarat* (darken) is to be gloomy, muddy or grimy. The word implies uncleanliness, ill health, and depression. The stars are depressed and darkened, that is to say, they no longer function as they used to.

> And when the mountains are set in motion, (at-takwir:3)

Even the mountains are moved along. Although they appeared solid – though even now they are not solid for they are always moving – they will have their movement enhanced to the point of collapse, and therefore, will disappear.

> And when the camels are left untended, (at-Takwir:4)

'*Ishar* are she-camels when ten months pregnant: they symbolize the main capital the Arabs had. '*Uttilat* (left untended) means that these prized possessions of the Arabs will be neglected and left alone. When the earth comes to an end, one will no longer tend to what was of value to him before. That former system of ecology will have ceased to function.

> And when the wild animals are herded together, (at-Takwir:5)

Wuhush are wild animals, and wild animals do not normally want to be collected together. This indicates that the former patterns of life no longer hold. What were once roaming wild, scattering as wild beasts do, are now gathered. At this stage another mechanism is at work. Mulla Sadra, may Allah have mercy upon him, said, in reference to this *ayah*, that it referred to human beings, for the beasts in us are shown clearly on that day.

Another great shaykh once said that if one were to look inside most people, one would find either asses, dogs, or wolves. Every one of us has predominating animal *nafs* (lower self). All the outer animals are there too, but one of them predominates. Animals do not only exist outside of oneself. Great movements of the pre-Islamic period often based their teachings on overcoming the dog or the pig in oneself. One can still find pictures of chariots drawn by a dog and a pig – wallowing in one's filth and thriving on it are the characteristics of the lower *nafs*.

> And when the seas are set on fire, (at-Takwir:6)

Two opposites, fire and water, will be brought together. One can imagine the fire to be volcanoes erupting from the sea. This *ayah*, like many others, emphasizes the fact that our present natural ecosystems will cease to function according to the laws of creation as we have known them. Fire and water, once the enemies of each other, are brought together and unified in a blaze.

> And when the female infant buried alive is asked for what sin she was killed, and when the books of (men's deeds) are spread, and when the heaven has its covering removed, and when the hell is fiercely kindled up, and when the garden is brought near, every soul shall (then) know what it has put forward. (at-Takwir:8-14)

These *ayat* are about the majority of people who are in doubt. Most of us lack `*ilm al-yaqin*, the knowledge of certainty that everything is already done and written in the book. On the micro level the book will unfold in our lives, and on the macro level, in the journey of the universe.

On that day of resurrection everything will be resurrected. The burying of female infants was a cultural habit of the Arabs and other peoples before the advent of Islam. This was done for various reasons, one being fear of provision, another was fear of dishonor by the female. By interfering with nature, with the highest of creation – which is man and his offspring – one is playing God. People who do such things do not see themselves in this life being judged by the Creator, so they take on the role of the Creator, and Giver and Taker of life, into their own hands. If they accept that the purpose of creation is to single-pointedly go through trials and tribulations in a state of worship and acceptance of what is in front of them, they will cease to act unjustly.

Elsewhere in the Qur'an it says: *yawma tashhadu `alayhim alsinatuhum wa aydihim wa arjuluhum bi-ma kanu ya`malun*, "On the day when their tongues and their hands and their feet shall bear witness against them as to what they did" (*an-Nur*:24). Man's every action and intention will leave its trace somewhere. They are the witnesses. Witnesses are not in the form of people coming up to the witness stand to testify. In this existence energies can only manifest in a form. In the next experience it is the reverse. Nothing will escape; everything will be brought forth. Here we can say it is unimportant, but we cannot really tell because the value system behind the coming judgment is based on another system, on ultimate justice, truthfulness, and honesty.

> And when the trumpet is blown with a single blast, and the earth and the mountains are borne away and crushed with a single crushing. On that day shall the great event come to pass, And the heavens shall cleave asunder, so that on that day it shall be frail. (al-Haqqah:13-16)

Just as the acceleration of creation was so fast and explosive to begin with, so too will the coming of the end be rapidly hastened on. The heavens will just crack. The mountains will explode and drift away like tufts of cotton. Everything as we know it will collapse, as though reverting backward in time, returning to the eternal void.

This scenario is one with which we cannot be familiar. We cannot imagine it in its magnitude for it is a unique event. All the natural laws and forces we know of seem to be ineffectual and out of order when the new phase of existence sets in.

> So when the sight becomes dazed, (al-Qiyamah:7)

Barq is lightning or flashes of light. *Al-Buraq* was the name of the horse on which the Prophet Muhammad made his ascension into the seven heavens. The name, *al-Buraq*, derives from the same root as *barq*. This implies that the horse moved faster than light. The Prophet's journey was completed in an instant, and an instant is beyond time.

The end will likewise come in a flash because it is closer in nature to timelessness. Timelessness was the state that existed before creation; from it rose creation and the experience of time. When the end comes, living beings will be dazed by the instantaneous transformation.

> And the moon becomes dark, and the sun and the moon are brought together, (al-Qiyamah:8-9)

As creation expanded outwardly, it will collapse on itself. *Khasafa* is to sink down, to disappear, to give away. *Khusuf* is a lunar eclipse. The moon collapsing means it is no longer what it was during the time in which it used to reflect the light of the sun. Its usual pattern of existence is destroyed.

Just as it was before creation when the sun and moon were in oneness, so they will once again reunite, because the end is the day of gathering – *yawm al-hashr*. What appears to be in dispersion now is, in reality, in gatheredness. In this existence there is an apparent dispersion which arises from the confusion of duality. When this experience of the cosmos comes to an end, creation will collapse back into its oneness. Confusion and discord will disappear; unity and harmony will prevail.

> Man shall say on that day; Whither to flee to? By no means! There shall be no place of refuge! With your Lord alone shall on that day be the place of rest. (al-Qiyamah:10-12)

On that day each individual will be confronted with the truth of what he had thought to be his own separate existence. He had thought that there existed a me and a you, a him and Allah. But now, on this day, everything is in gatheredness; separation no longer exists. The bewilderment is so engulfing that every self will only be concerned with its own reality.

CHAPTER 6: THE FINAL COLLAPSE

The final resting place is with the Lord, the Sustainer, Who has brought this creation to its fullness and now to its greater fullness in another guise. *Mustaqarr*, resting place, is derived from *qarra*, to settle, and also, to decide, to make a statement. There is no longer the possibility of confused questioning as to "why?" or about the apparent duality of this existence.

> Man shall on that day be informed of what he sent before and (what he) put off. (al-Qiyamah:13)

To inform, *naba'a*, is the job of the *nabiyy*, the one who gives the news, the Prophet. It is he who tells us now of what is going to happen when each of us will know what he has put into his life and what he has postponed, when he will truly come to know himself. That is why we say he who knows himself now knows his Lord.

We are informed that the way towards knowledge of the self is through recognition of the lower self. That recognition itself will adjust one's turning more towards the higher self, and one will then begin to experience higher consciousness. One will have a clearer understanding of events that occur outside of oneself and of happenings that occur inside of one, as well as the relationship between the two. Man will be closer to the knowledge of *tawhid*.

> Nay! Man is evidence against himself, though he puts forth his excuses. (al-Qiyamah:14-15)

At all times man is a witness of himself. He has the capacity to witness because he has within him the light of consciousness, even though he may constantly give excuses. If he could see why he tries to justify his choices and actions, that perception would actually sharpen the light of his consciousness. If he could only admit that he is avoiding the truth because of his selfish habits – if he could just say, "I have to have my coffee, I'm used to it and I'm enslaved by the habit" – there is a chance of him being cured. Otherwise, he will constantly defend himself and continue with the excuses of the *nafs*.

> Therefore keep watch for the day when the heaven shall bring forth an evident smoke that shall overtake men; this is a painful punishment. (ad-Dukhan:10-11)

Dukhan in Arabic is vapor or smoke. Earlier on we described the heavens and earth as one subtle, vaporous mass; the end is similarly described. For those who deny the truth that this existence is only a temporary one, the Qur'an says to wait until the day comes when smoke will be evident. The entire creation will go up in smoke, and this existence will revert to its plasmic, primordial state. After the big collapse that solidity, that certainty, that physicality will return to its most vaporous state.

> On the day when the heaven shall be as molten copper, and the mountains shall be as tufts of wool, and friend shall not ask of friend. (al-Ma`arij:8-10)

On that day the heavens and the mountains will regress from their solidity into fluidity and beyond – they will become mirages. That, in fact, is the reality of their present state, but the faculty of *khayal* (imagination) we think they are solid. That is why the more we scientifically penetrate that solidity, the more we find that there are no building blocks as such, only dynamism. Dynamism is the trick of time.

Solidity is like *shari`ah* (revealed Islamic law or code of conduct). From there we have to move towards its counterpart, *haqiqah* (inner truth). You cannot move inwardly unless you are polished outwardly. If you start purifying your outermost – your clothes, your skin, your food and so on – you will finally come to your innermost. But in our mad culture we stop half-way. We only tend to the outer cosmetics, caring little about what is inside. Everything is based on appearance. As long as the house looks nice and there is a floodlight on the tree and a bit of fancy flora around, it is acceptable. That is our reality. We have beautiful highways and picnic grounds, but if one could just peek into the hearts of those who are picnicking, then one would see something else. One would find that the outer grooming does not continue towards the inner. It stops short. Had it continued, then it would have reached deep inside and would have unified – *tawhid*.

Man starts with the outer and ends up with the inner. If he begins with *shari`ah* and moves on rather than stops, he will arrive at *haqiqah*. And if he begins with *haqiqah*, rebelling against everything, he will end up in *shari`ah*. He will find that he has to constrict himself in order to be able to interact correctly and share what he thereby gains with others. If there is no outer containment, how can a community grow? How can there be interaction? How can there be Madinah?

Hamim is an intimate friend, the root of which is *hamma*, to heat or warm up. Friendship means being warm with each other. *Hammam*, bath, is from the same root; and the traditional baths of the east were always warm. The implication is that unification comes about when there is fusion, and one can fuse two things together only when one warms them. One cannot connect their different elements unless one puts them in a pot and heats them up. The key here is alchemy. Heat makes the molecules more mobile so they can intermingle – that is friendship.

> Surely hell lies in wait, a place of return for the transgressors. (an-Naba:21-22)

The next occurrence is the resurrection. With the resurrection there is *jannah* (gardens of paradise) and *jahannam* (hell), and between them there will be a clear division.

Jahannam, the bottomless pit, is the place of return for the *taghin*, the transgressors, which they themselves were already digging during this life. If someone digs a grave for others – plotting against them and planning their downfall – it will become his grave, his own plot. Since everything is in *tawhid* (divine unity), each individual is the culmination of his actions, which by inevitable extension, means that he is as good as his intentions. There is no separation.

> Requital corresponding (to their sins). (an-Naba':26)

Wifaq (corresponding) is from *wafaqa*, to be suitable, appropriate or consistent. The word implies, harmony, although in this world we may not see the harmonious reward of the transgressors. Throughout the ages, and also in the Qur'an, we find some prophets wondering why the transgressors live so well. The answer of Truth is that they are already in the fire, even though they may imagine it to be otherwise; and that is where they will be, both here and in the next life.

But this is not only about the next life. If one has wisdom and discrimination and can see someone overwhelming himself with luxuries and excess, the result is clear. He will become completely enslaved by what he is doing. Hundreds of people will come to him, like bees to honey, because he has the "goods". Everybody wants him, everybody loves him. With the eyes of wisdom, however, one can see at once that he is heading for trouble. Once there is the "I", arrogance arises, and one is with *shaytan*. God's mercy upon us is to show us the fire here and now. If we are close to nature, to Reality, we will begin to suffer from it now. The taste of the fire is God's mercy upon us so that we will turn away from bad action and question both our actions and intentions. In this manner we are returned to safety.

In the new life, the energy wavebands or entities that took on physical forms in this life will all manifest without their physical shells. Their manifestation will, however, be colored by their actions in this experience on earth. The Qur'an describes people as *suhufan munashsharah*, open books. The alphabet of man's character will no longer be hidden. The purity or impurity of his heart will be evident. He will not be able to conceal it behind a smile or behind the facade of immaculate dress.

On the Day of Judgment everything will be just. At the end of each day in this life man is precisely the direct result of what he made of himself. In the next life the reality behind the facade will be evident. People will recognize each other because they will still retain the form they had in this life, but what will dominate will be their inner reality. In this life what dominates is our physical reality; we can hide our inner reality. The mirror image will be in reverse. In the non-time zone every individual will continuously be the exact sum of what he made himself to be when he existed in time. If he has evolved and brought himself up to his divine reality, the ultimate truthfulness of His Creator, then his eternal state will reflect that.

La yamuta fiha wala yahya; "He shall not die therein, nor shall he live" (*Ta Ha*:74). In the fire there is no life nor is there the release of death. *Jahannam* (hell) is like a bottomless pit. It is like falling down an endless tunnel, like being in a state of alarm, fright, and heart-wrenching suspense. The fire is like that; as soon as one tries to be healed, one is burned again. The people of the garden, on the other hand, are in bliss, ever stable tranquility and peace. Any agitation or desire is instantly gratified. Perpetual and total peace reigns with conscious awareness – the purest form of life.

Chapter 7: Eternal Life

We have tried to pick the *ayat* which describe to us the meaning behind, as well as the form of, creation. We covered the description of the beginning of creation; how it arose from one unified field; how the earth and heavens then separated; how the earth became stabilized; and how life arose from it. In the meantime, we were given the parallel inner meaning of, and the reason for, the rise of man, and the fact that he must go through this purification, this inward melting pot of the world, so that the rise of higher consciousness takes place within him. With the development of intellect and awareness he gains the wisdom of discrimination that stems from the knowledge of *tawhid* – seeing two and glorifying One, seeing the good and bad, and knowing that all of it stems from the One.

> That I may do good in that which I have left. By no means! It is a mere word that he speaks; and before them is a barrier until the day they are raised. (al-Mu'minun:100)

As far as the individual is concerned, the end of his life experience comes with the unique breakthrough experience of death. For him, death represents his personal or mini-resurrection, because between that experience and resurrection he is suspended in a zone of non-time and non-action. Those who are still living call that space of time between an individual's death and everyone's final day a *barzakh*, an interval, gap, or a non-man's land. We remain in this *barzakh* until all life comes to an end and resurrection and its attendant states come about. Each of us will then enter only one experience of non-time, whether pleasant or unpleasant, garden-like or hellish.

Entering the *barzakh* involves breaking away from the past state of life on earth. In the *barzakh* one is unable to act or change everything in one's total record system. The new state of eternity has not yet come about, and there is an apparent waiting period, as if one is in no-man's land between two national borders. The end of this waiting period comes when all experiences of physical creation on earth come to an end – the big collapse – and when all living things are submerged again into the state of subtlety and thereby into another realm of existence that is completely beyond our intellectual capacity to comprehend.

At the end of the expanding big bang – as we have seen, everything is in expansion – a point will be reached when creation will collapse and revert to the zone of non-time, where time no longer exists as we experience it. Then we will go through the regeneration of the garden and the fire, and everyone will recognize that he has experienced these states before in the form of an echo, because the next life will be a reversed mirror image of this life. But because it is in a timeless zone it will be on a different level of consciousness. This is the message we receive from the Qur'an in describing the cosmic journey from which we are not separated.

Imam ʿAli, upon him be peace, said: "Your remedy is in you but you do not feel it and your illness is from you but you do not see it." Our illness is the illness of the *nafs*. Our illness is caused by a feeling of separation and disconnectedness. We are not in true submission. We are not in abandonment. We think there is something outside to study – "Islamic studies". One is either in Islam or he is studying it; and the lack of discrimination between the two is a subtler and more difficult madness to cure.

Islam is only meaningful in action and application. A teacher of Islam must, by definition, be an expert and an acknowledged practitioner, whose practice thereof evidently gives him wisdom and safe conduct. One never subjects oneself to a swimming instructor who has never swum, no matter how much an expert he may be on style and fitness.

Imam `Ali also said: "And you are the evident book and by its signs the hidden becomes evident." If one is a follower of the Prophet, peace and blessings be upon him, then he has to try to be the Book on two legs. He must take on the responsibility of following in the footsteps of the Messenger, and he too will reverberate and echo the message – to varying degrees of clarity, proportionate to the clarity of his mirror's reflection. If the mirror is not tarnished, if there is, as the sufi says, nothing of the individual left – if he has gone beyond *fana'* (self-obliteration) – then he is in the hand of *al-Baqi* (the Everlasting). Then he knows that he is a *fani* (one who has experienced *fana'*), that he has no real existence. What is hidden will be unveiled by his own inner signs, his actions, his *ayat*. One has only to look at a man of clarity to know who he is. One looks at what he does, how he eats, how he lives – his outward conduct is a result of his inward clarity. There is no separation.

The vessel will ooze what is within it. The contents will eventually reveal themselves. In these times, however, we are broken vessels. We are often not "ourselves"; that means we must be someone else. We have all become "cracked pots". That is why most of us have to be at the mercy of millions of psychoanalysts.

The purpose of creation is for us to realize that we encompass the Book. This is the decree, the law that governs this life and what is beyond it, whether we like it or not. Every action has an equal and opposite reaction – this is absolutely scientific. The seen and unseen laws that govern are superimposed upon each other in a multitudinal fashion. For this reason we are often confused and cannot see what the outcome of certain actions will be, because we have a limited capacity to compute. We are, in a sense, confused. But if we have *iman*, trust, we take what is in front of us, and we will see that there is enough for us for the time being.

Allah says: "The heavens and the earth do not contain *Me* but the heart of a *mu'min* (believer) contains *Me*." The knowledge or reality, of Allah, is potentially there. But we have built different layers of our own expectations, fears, desires, and anxieties. The intake of our perception is filtered through these various layers of our *nafs*, so we can only see everything in a distorted fashion.

We now come to the last point of this straight path. How can we recognize anything outside unless its seed is within us? How can we recognize the virtue of generosity unless the meaning and taste of generosity is within us, as well as the recognition that it is virtuous? It would otherwise be impossible.

The whole process of spiritual evolution begins by awareness of Allah, by remembrance of Allah. The mind creates all sorts of questions and problems by not being in *dhikr* (awareness, remembrance). With pure awareness, the heart begins to be anchored, to be content, sure, and tranquil. From that tranquility, one suddenly realizes that the Book is there, and he reads. One should read what is easy for him, what is of use to him there and then. He should read it with the courtesy of the Prophet, peace and blessings be upon him: absorb from the Qur'an what is easiest to absorb at the time of reading – "Read what is easy of the Qur'an" (*al-Muzammil*:20). The meaning will come to him if he has trust. Allah will give him the knowledge. A full life is based on trust. Man is the Book and whatever he needs of the Book.

"Do not move your tongue with it to make haste with it" (*al-Qiyamah*:15). Do not hurry it up. Allah is beyond time and there is only Allah. If one thinks there is other than Allah, it is an illusion that has to be discarded by being still, by dwelling in that inner abandonment. In that abandonment, when the mercy befalls him, man will see the visible abundance, which is of no consequence anyway. All the fruits are near, so what does one do? He will take some for what he needs at the time and move on along this apparent framework called time, so that he reaches into the timeless zone from where he has originated.

How can there be time unless there is no time? How can there be man without woman? How can there be goodness without badness? How can there be existence without non-existence? How can there be this life unless there is a next life? Our path is the only path, the path of knowledge that is within each heart. Other aspects of knowledge are informational, existential, encyclopedic, useful. We need them to make our life sufficiently smooth so that we may move on and recognize the great gift that is given to us. Skills, however are not real knowledge.

> O soul that has inner peace! Return to your Lord, well-pleased (with Him), well-pleasing Him. (al-Fajr:27-28)

Return to where? Your Lord is already there. He is not somewhere else, sitting on a chair or a "throne" as the word is mistranslated from `arah. `Arsh is like the foundation of a house, the structure upon which everything is built. The `arsh is the building block of this construction.

Imagine, then, that man is a tiny planet and that in him is folded up – encapsulated, genetically encoded – the entire cosmos. Similarly, man contains within himself the seed of all things. How can one relate to something unless its seed is in each one of us? It is not possible, unless the entire spectrum of all the creational colors is in us. All the eye does is capture the light and send it through so that it unifies with that primal record, the Book in us.

With that, man will have inward certainty about the meaning of this journey. It starts with *`ilm al-yaqin*, the knowledge of certainty. It then progresses to *`ayn al-yaqin*, the eye of certainty – when he begins to see it reflecting within. And then he reaches *haqq al-yaqin*, the truth of certainty. Once that stage is reached, there will be nothing else that can change it. He can do nothing other than be a true slave, and his freedom rises from the experiential recognition of his slavehood.

There is no choice. Man is totally and absolutely stuck with the One. Recognition of this is the cause of his rise. Such is the love of the Creator for His created. For this reason, we have been given the opportunity of this lifetime. A lifetime is only one day, like the day of reckoning, but it is stretched differently – 50,000 years away or one day, it is still a period of time. If one is willing and able to stop everything outwardly, then he will have a glimpse of the inner record.

We are that record, whether we like it or not. Confusion is there because we are not unified. We have divided for information's sake – this is my work, that is his, etc. Reality, however, is permeated by Oneness. Throughout our life we seek to unify, to interrelate and correlate. All our sciences clumsily attempt to interconnect various subsystems in this one, all-encompassing all-engulfing perfection. Confusion occurs because we do not trust that all is held together by one fiber, be it invisible or visible, subtle or physical.

From weakness comes strength. From death comes life. If we want to experience that next life, the passage to it is to experience death in this life, and that comes through utter and absolute silence. It comes by the practice of *muraqabah* (meditative observation), by the *shari`ah* practices of *i`tikaf* (seclusion). *Shari`ah* and *haqiqah* are one. We divide them only in order to talk about them. Look at the beauty and perfection: *shari`ah* will lead you to *haqiqah*. *Haqiqah* will lead you to *shari`ah*.

CHAPTER 7: ETERNAL LIFE

And Allah will lead you to Allah.

Everything man thinks has taken place in this existence can only have been experienced because the dynamic flux of life in time was reflected upon the unchanging, ever-steady, primal state within him. The search for knowledge, love of the familiar, enmity, fear, and dislike of what we do not know, love of tranquility and harmony – all these directing factors in our lives are there because there is within us a continuously repeating reminder of complete and true submission with knowledge to the one and only Reality.

The entire cosmos follows its unfolding path along its journey through time with complete loyalty. Within this greater journey, man is given the freedom to recognize the rules of his journey and to apply them by his faculty of discriminating reason. If both the universe and the highest intelligence living in it are destined to follow the known and unknown laws of creation, the end to their journey is clear. During his lifetime, man's very own nature encourages him to cast his vision further afield that his day to day animalistic existence, beyond the horizon of time. It is only by keeping to the divine path that he will be able to use this time efficiently, resourcefully and rewardingly. The nature and rules of this journey were decided upon before the consciousness of his existence arose. Man has no choice but to abandon himself and travel along the perfect path towards his destiny.

Glossary

The following is an expanded glossary of the key Arabic terms used by the author, arranged according to the English alphabet. Transliteration used throughout this book is based on the American Library of Congress system.

Allah – God; literally "the God"; the name that designates the source from which all things seen and unseen emanate. The name Allah encompasses all the Divine Names, such as, *ar-Rahman*, the Beneficent, and *al-`Alim*, the Knower (of all things).

`aql* – Faculty of reason, intelligence, discernment, rationality, mind, intellect; from the verb *`aqala, to keep back (a camel by tying its foreleg), to detain, confine, to be restricted, be reasonable, understand, have intelligence, realize. This implies that true reason and intelligence can only be realized by keeping back the lower self (see *nafs*).

`arsh* – Usually translated as throne, also means foundation, support, and by implication, control; supports something which on its own will not grow or survive. Verbal root is *`arasha, to construct, build houses, support. *`Arish* is a trellis (vine).

ayah, ayat – Qur'anic verse/verses; sign/signs or mark.

barzakh – Interval, gap; interspace or suspension of time into which all beings enter after death. They remain in this state, awaiting entry into eternity, until the entire physical universe has come to an end. As a living being, man is also considered a *barzakh*, an interspace between the visible and invisible realms.

dhikr – Remembrance or awareness of Allah which can be stimulated by the invocations of His Divine Names and other formulae from the Qur'an and sayings of the Prophet and his beloved family. From the verb *dhakara*, to remember, think, to relate. Derivations include *mudhakkir*, one who reminds himself (thereby admonishing himself), and *dhakar*, male.

din – Usually translated to mean religion, the word strongly implies transaction between the Debtor (Allah) and the indebted (man), because the verbal root is *dana*, to owe, be indebted to, take a loan, to be inferior. Hence, living the *din* means repaying one's debt to the Creator, or indeed, behaving as befits the high station of man in creation.

fitnah – Temptation, trial; attractiveness, enchantment, and captivation. *Fitnah* is whatever distracts and disturbs. It also means, therefore, riot, discord, and civil strife. The purpose of *fitnah* is to show the true nature of what is being afflicted. From the verb *fatana*, to try, tempt, seduce, afflict, torment.

furqan – Discrimination (faculty thereof), distinction, proof, evidence; epithet of the Qur'an, because it distinguishes true from false. Derives from the verb *faraqa*, to separate, divide, make a distinction, discriminate (between), be afraid.

ghaflah – Heedlessness, carelessness, negligence, foolishness, stupidity; from the verb *ghafala*, to ignore, neglect, disregard.

hadith – Tradition, saying (usually of the Prophet, relating his deeds and utterances); speech, account, narrative. From the verb *hadatha*, to happen, be new; and *haddatha*, to relate, report, speak about.

haqiqah – Truth, fact, reality; the true nature of creation. From the verb *haqqa*, to be true, right, just.

`ibadah* – Worship, devotion, adoration, service (of and to Allah); religious observances. From the verb *`abada, to serve, worship, adore. *`Abd* is one who is totally devoted to God. *`Abbada* is to make smooth or passable for traffic – by complete and utter devotion to Allah, man's passage through life is made smooth.

iman – Faith, trust, belief; from the verb *amana.*, to believe (in). Other words from the same root are: *amina*, to be secure, to trust; *amn*, peace, security, protection; *amin* (designation of the Prophet), trustworthy, faithful, loyal, honest; *mu'min*, believing, faithful.

jahannam – Hell, burning fire; not only of the next life, but of this life as well.

jihad – Literally, striving (for the sake of Allah); fighting so-called Holy War, for the sake of establishing truth and justice in an unbalanced situation. From the verb *jahada*, to endeavor, strive, do one's utmost, expend energy.

kafir, kuffar – Denier (of the existence of Allah), one who covers up (the truth), ingrate; from the verb *kafara*, to cover, hide, be ungrateful, not to believe.

kufr – Denial, unbelief, ingratitude (see *kafir*).

Mahdi – Rightly guided; the twelfth Imam (leader) from the family of the Prophet Muhammad. He is not apparent now but will return when all the signs related to the body of *hadith* have come to pass so as to destroy man's injustice and establish a state based on worship and divine justice. The arrival of the *Mahdi* will herald the beginning of the last stage of creation. From the verb *hada*, to lead on the right way, guide, to show (the right way).

mizan – Balance, weight, measure; *al-Mizan*, epithet of the Qur'an. From the verb *wazana*, to balance, weigh, equilibrate, even up.

mu'min – Believing, faithful; believer (see *iman*).

nafs – Self, soul, mind, human being. The *nafs* includes man's innate nature, his genetic predisposition, and his conditioned behavior. Its manifestation may be base and animalistic, or spiritually elevated, according to the state of its purity. From the verb *nafusa*, to be precious, valuable. It is also related to *naffasa*, to cheer up, reassure, relieve; and *tanaffasa*, to breathe, inhale, pause for a rest.

Rabb – Lord, Master, Sustainer; from the verb, *rabba*, to be master, lord, possessor of, and *rabbaba*, to bring up, raise. The Lord is that entity which brings its subject up to its full potential. Related to it is *rububiyyah*, lordship, divinity.

rahmah – Mercy, kindness, compassion; from the verb, *rahima*, to be merciful, have mercy upon. Derived from this root are the following: *ar-Rahman*, the Beneficent, and *ar-Rahim*, the Merciful, both attributes of Allah. *Rahim*, meaning womb or kinship, implies that through these His mercy is ever-present, nurturing and sustaining.

ruh – Spirit, soul; from the verb *raha*, to go away, leave, begin, set out. Derived from this root are the following: *rawwaha*, to refresh, relax, rest; *arwaha*, to release, relieve, sooth; *istarwaha*, to breathe, smell, be refreshed, be calm, happy, glad; *rih*, wind; *Ruhu-llah*, spirit of Allah, a title given to particularly pious and ascetic people such as the Prophet Jesus.

shari`ah* – Revealed Islamic law or code of conduct, outward path; from the verb *shara`a, to begin, enter, unbind, introduce, prescribe, give (laws). *Shari`* means road or spring. It is the complement and container of *haqiqah* (see *haqiqah*), for the waters that gush from Reality's spring cannot be contained or drunk from except by a proper vessel.

shaytan – Satan, devil; that entity or force which causes one to transgress. *Shaytan* is from within and without. From the verb *shatana*, to be obstinate, perverse; to be cast off (a path); to fasten, bind.

shirk – Associating other-than-Allah with Allah, idolatry, polytheism; from the verb *sharika*, to be a companion, to share, participate, associate. A *mushrik* perpetuates this association.

shukr – Gratitude, thankfulness, praise; from the verb *shakara*, to give thanks, be grateful, to praise. Often used in antithesis of

GLOSSARY

kufr (see *kufr*).

sunnah – Way, habitual custom, line of conduct; used in reference to Allah or the Prophet. From the verb *sanna*, to shape, form, prescribe, enact, establish.

surah – Chapter of the Qur'an, sign, degree of rank; from the verb, *sara*, to mount a wall; or *sawwara*, to enclose, fence in.

taqwa – Fearful awareness, devoutness; from the verb *waqa*, to guard, preserve, shield, shelter, protect, prevent (a danger).

tawhid – Divine unity, union; belief in Allah's oneness. From the verb *wahada*, to be alone, unique, singular, unmatched, without equal. Derivations include: *wahhada*, to unite, unify, connect, join, profess belief in the oneness of God; *wahdah*, oneness, singleness, seclusion, self-containment; *al-Wahid*, the One; *al-Ahad*, the Singular without number (attribute of Allah).

yawm – Day, era, age, time; period of time. From the verb *yawima*, to be or exist for a day (period of time). *Yawm al-qiyamah, yawm al-fasl, yawm ad-din*, are all epithets of the Day of Resurrection or Judgment, and are not necessarily the days but the time in which resurrection will occur.

www.ingramcontent.com/pod-product-compliance
Lightning Source LLC
Chambersburg PA
CBHW070620050426
42450CB00011B/3090